IMAGES
of America

FOLEY

BALDWIN COUNTY HISTORICAL MAP. Baldwin County has a colorful history springing from its location on Mobile Bay, Perdido Bay, and the Gulf of Mexico. This map, drawn by Walter Overton, highlights the colorful history of the southernmost county in Alabama. (Courtesy of Baldwin County Department of Archives and History.)

ON THE COVER: LOUISVILLE & NASHVILLE DEPOT. The town of Foley grew as the result of a spur rail line built running south from the L&N line in Bay Minette. The depot shown on the cover was built in 1909 after the first one burned in 1908. (Courtesy of Foley Museum.)

IMAGES
of America

FOLEY

Harriet Brill Outlaw and Penny H. Taylor

ARCADIA
PUBLISHING

Published by Arcadia Publishing
Charleston, South Carolina

Library of Congress Control Number: 2012954451

For all general information, please contact Arcadia Publishing:
Telephone 843-853-2070
Fax 843-853-0044
E-mail sales@arcadiapublishing.com
For customer service and orders:
Toll-Free 1-888-313-2665

Visit us on the Internet at www.arcadiapublishing.com

For our families, who work as hard as we do on our projects

CONTENTS

ACKNOWLEDGMENTS

As in any work of this nature, the authors are deeply indebted to many people who have generously given of their time and knowledge. During the process of collecting information on the Foley area, many local experts have emerged to contribute to the body of information contained in this book. Each community has at least one historian who is dedicated to the preservation of the community story. In the city of Foley, the city museum is a treasure trove of memorabilia of the town. The museum, located in the depot shown on the cover of this book, is under the direction of Bonnie Cleaveland, who opened her doors and heart to assist in the process. Doris Rich wrote the history of Foley through 1921, and her son Tom Stoddard completed the anecdotal history of the town after 1921. Both volumes provide the information needed to identify most of the photographs of early Foley—all which would have been lost without their efforts. Jeannette Bornholt, a native whose dedication to preservation of local history is evidenced in the collection she has compiled in the library, manages the Genealogical Research Room at the Foley Public Library.

Just east of Foley, the Baldwin County Heritage Museum, in the town of Elberta, houses an immense collection of artifacts depicting the growth of the entire county. Local residents June Taylor and museum manager Tammy Kenney have already compiled excellent booklets and scrapbooks telling the story of the settlers of Elberta, many of whom were of German descent. West of town, in the newly incorporated town of Magnolia Springs, the city hall is making a herculean effort to collect the photographs and anecdotes of one of the earliest communities of the area. Special thanks go to the Magnolia Springs Heritage Club, which prints the local cookbook full of wonderful stories of the river town. Volunteers at the Weeks Bay National Estuarine Research Reserve on Fish River have tirelessly collected and documented photographs particular to the area drained by Weeks Bay. The authors are also very appreciative of the Baldwin County Historical Development Commission for permission to use the photographs at the Swift-Coles Historic Home in Bon Secour. Bon Secour history is also preserved by Ione Swift Jurkiewicz, Jeannie Collins, Mary Beth Hayes, and the Nelson family, who have all shared their memories and photographs.

The authors appreciate this opportunity to say "Thank you" to all who make that extra effort to keep our heritage alive.

INTRODUCTION

Today, the city of Foley, Alabama, is dubbed the Forward City, and it has lived up to that name since its earliest days. Sometimes considered the gateway to resort beaches of Gulf Shores and the surrounding communities, its heritage is distinct in its own right. When water travel was the primary mode of transportation, the landings at Miflin and Bon Secour were the main accesses to the land in the center of the county. But with the completion of the railway spur line in 1905, nearby land became most desirable. Foley owes its development to the foresight of those investors who acquired large portions of land to parcel and sell to home-seekers. J.B. Foley, a Chicago businessman who traveled regularly to the sunny South in the early 1900s, was one of the primary leaders in the movement to create a community in the rural area. He laid out streets in the early town, and businesses grew at a rapid rate. Most of the early settlers migrated south from the Midwest, where advertisements touting the perfect farming and living conditions in south Alabama ran in newspapers.

Early town history centers around the Foley depot, which is today's city museum. The home-seeker excursions ran every first and third Wednesday to transport would-be farmers to explore the possibilities in the area. Hotels such as the Magnolia were built to house the future farmers, businessmen, and vacationers. Agents were on hand to meet future residents at the depot to show town lots and the opportunities awaiting them in the fertile farmlands nearby.

As the town grew, J.B. Foley continued to contribute to the future of the residents by donating land for schools and for any religious group to build a church. By 1912, there were four churches and a three-room schoolhouse. Town leaders were visionaries, especially concerning education. Since the school system could only fund wooden buildings, local leaders signed notes to build a two-story building, which became known throughout Alabama as the finest school in the state, in 1916. As was typical in Alabama, children of African American descent attended separate schools during the first half of the 20th century. The residents of Aaronville built a school for the neighborhood children in grades one through seven. However, students continuing their high school education attended a boarding school in Daphne, the only county high school for black students until 1950, when a high school was built in Bay Minette. From 1950 until Aaronville High School was built in 1960, black high school students were transported by bus to Daphne. Aaronville High School was in operation until schools were integrated in 1970.

After the rail line provided efficient means of transportation, Foley became a hub for several nearby towns. East of Foley, a farming community developed by the Baldwin County Colonization Company attracted many families of German descent beginning in 1903. The Old World heritage has been preserved there to a remarkable degree.

West of Foley is the beautiful town of Magnolia Springs, which preceded Foley in growth due to the beautiful spring-fed river and the resort homes and hotels built along its banks. The Woodbound Hotel and the Governor's Club were resorts extraordinaire, and many Northerners spent summers on the banks of the scenic river.

The community of Bon Secour on the Bon Secour River is one of the earliest settlements in Alabama, being the resting place for French explorers who stopped there to weather a storm and named it "Safe Harbor." Many French descendants have since called it home, as has the Swift family, which moved to Bon Secour and established a lumber mill there. The famous Meme's Restaurant was on the grounds of the Big House, as the Swift home was fondly dubbed. Fisheries such as Nelson's, Shutt's, and Aquilla's have flourished there since the earliest days, and oyster boats and shrimpers have always been a common sight on the Bon Secour River.

Agriculture was king in Baldwin County, and the south part of the county was the throne. Here were massive citrus farms until the freeze of 1935 destroyed most of that industry, which was soon replaced by a thriving flower industry. Fields of gladioli were common sights along the rural dirt roads, and special boxcars were designed to transport the cut flowers to market. An ice compartment at the end of the wooden boxcar was filled at the depot in Foley. Potatoes were also a major crop due to the early harvest possible in the warm climate. Potato sheds were located at every stop on the rail line.

The World War II era brought change, and patriotism was evidenced throughout the town. Barin Field, the naval aviation training base; nearby Fort Morgan; and Pensacola Naval Air Station were in full operation. The USO Club was housed in the downtown building that is now the Gift Horse Restaurant. Here, the local residents entertained military personnel, and many a romance began at the regular Saturday night dances. This was also the era in which the law enforcement personnel were increased, and B.D. Cobb began his 30-year tenure as chief of police.

The 1950s were years of glory for the town. The Foley High School football team was Alabama State Champions in 1961 and 1962 under the coaching of legendary Ivan Jones. Teenagers were driving cars to the Hang Out at the Gulf, and the Dairy Queen was the place to be seen. Students from Gulf Shores and Orange Beach attended school at Foley, and the community virtually included all people south of Robertsdale.

Hurricane Frederic in 1979 brought total destruction to most of the area. However, it must have put south Baldwin on the radar, because a tremendous growth spurt occurred in the 1980s. The population grew exponentially, and the town of Foley continued to live up to its name, the Forward City.

One

FOUNDING FOLEY

FIRST SCHOOLHOUSE. The first schoolhouse for the town children was built in 1905 and was used as a school during the week and for church meetings on Sundays. The first teacher was Edna Peadro; she was paid $42.65 per month and boarded with local families. In 1917, it was moved about five blocks next to the new two-story high school, where it was used for elementary classes. (Courtesy of Baldwin County Heritage Museum.)

FIRST TRAIN DEPOT. The spur line running from Bay Minette southward to Foley was completed on May 11, 1905. The depot pictured here was ready to meet the train on its maiden journey. The Ham brothers and John B. Foley, the owner of the Magnolia Springs Land Company, built the line. They contracted with the Louisville & Nashville Railroad (L&N) to operate the trains on the line. This depot burned in 1908. (Courtesy of Foley Museum.)

PINE KNOT SPECIAL. A devastating hurricane in 1906 left 119 casualties and miles of pinewood in the fields. The L&N converted a steam engine to burn pine by modifying the smokestack and covering it with a screen to keep burning embers from escaping. Wood was gathered by local residents and piled in boxes along the track. S.J. Feagin, engineer, is pictured on the left. (Courtesy of Foley Museum.)

1909 DEPOT. Soon after the first depot burned, a new and expanded building was constructed in Foley at the end of the Bay Minette and Fort Morgan line branch. J.B. Foley, a Chicago businessman and president of Foley and Company, which produced medicines, printing, and engraving, founded the town. He started the Magnolia Springs Land Company and purchased 40,000 acres near the terminus of the rail line. (Courtesy of Foley Museum.)

FIRST STORE IN TOWN. The first store, pictured above, was owned and operated by W.H. Montieth, who had come to Magnolia Springs from Iowa about 1898. He moved to Foley about 1902 and started the post office in this store after the railroad line was completed in 1905. Until the rail line was done, all goods were shipped on roads from Magnolia Springs or Miflin boat landings. (Courtesy of Foley Museum.)

CALLING ALL HOME-SEEKERS. Land developers and real estate agents such as P.J. Cooney advertised widely throughout the Midwest. Home-seekers were given tours of successful farms of the earliest settlers, such as F.W. Kuhn, G.L. Barnes, H.J. Williamson, Richard Coesens, and M.S. Dreitzler, who had moved their families to 50-acre farms in 1905. They shipped their first produce the following year. (Courtesy of Harriet Brill Outlaw.)

PLANK SIDEWALKS. Early reports of the town indicate that most of it was still swamp, so the town built wooden plank sidewalks. J.B. Foley had the streets surveyed in 1903 by J.R. McKenzie, for whom the main north-south street was named. By 1912, Foley had built sawmills, sugar mills, and an experimental farm. (Courtesy of Swift-Coles Historic Home.)

STOREFRONTS IN TOWN. Several real estate agents built offices such as the one pictured above near the depot. They were on hand to greet would-be residents. They offered transportation, a night's boarding, and a tour of available land. It was here that the Stelk brothers built their first store, as seen on the right. They later constructed a two-story brick building on the southwest corner of the main intersection in town (State Bank of Foley and later Wright's Drugs). (Courtesy of Baldwin County Heritage Museum.)

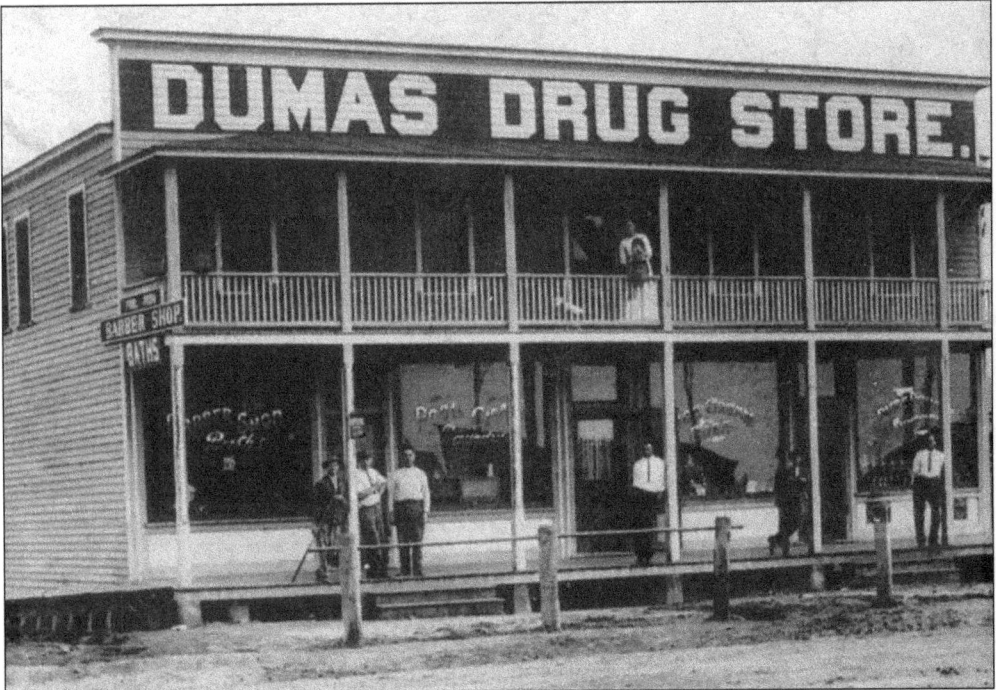

DUMAS DRUGS. James Dumas, a young druggist and violinist, was charmed by the prospects in the Zenith City, as promoters dubbed the new town, and built one of the first pharmacies. This building was on the southwest corner of Alston Street and Laurel Avenue. It was later moved to the diagonal lot by rolling it on logs. Dumas served as mayor from 1920 through 1924. (Courtesy of Foley Museum.)

CHICAGO STREET. Looking south on Chicago Street from Laurel Avenue, the first building nearest the depot was the Harmony Hotel. The next building to the left has a sign above the door that reads, "Restaurant. Meals at all hours." The post office is next in the row, followed by a building labeled STAR. Chicago Street is the first street east of the railroad tracks. (Courtesy of Foley Museum.)

BOLLER'S AND FESLER'S. The building on the left of the storefronts pictured above is the Charles Boller Merchandise Store, which he purchased from builder H.J. Coenen in 1908. The next building is a real estate office, and the third is a two-story building erected by Frank Fesler, the publisher the first newspaper in Foley, the *Onlooker*, which was located in the downstairs. Fesler's family lived upstairs, where his daughter, the first child in Foley, was born. The Hotel Magnolia is on the far right. (Courtesy of Baldwin County Heritage Museum.)

HOTEL MAGNOLIA. John Foley started the Hotel Magnolia, built of heart pine, just west of the depot in 1907; it opened its doors to the public in 1908. The first manager was John Lehr, who made the hotel the social center of town. His daughter Marie played piano music in the evenings. The windmill was added in 1909 to provide running water and plumbing to the hotel. (Courtesy of John Lewis.)

ONLOOKER OFFICE. The *Onlooker* was first published by Frank Fesler, who moved the office from his home to a block bungalow north on McKenzie Street. N.V. Lillard purchased the paper in 1918 but soon sold it to Frank Barchard. The paper operated from this bungalow for more than 50 years. (Courtesy of Foley Museum.)

RAILROAD WORKERS. A section crew maintained the track and yard. Trains here turned around on the wye, a formation of the tracks allowing the engines to reverse without a turntable. Section houses built nearby for workers also served as temporary housing for future home owners. From left to right are unidentified, Charlie Dunson, Bester Johnson, Ollie Presley, and Dock F. Pippin, section foreman from 1926 to 1953. (Courtesy of Foley Museum.)

HUBERT C. PIPPIN
Yardman / Engineer

LOCOMOTIVE ENGINEER. Hubert C. Pippin, yardman and engineer, was a well-known engineer who regularly ran the Bay Minette to Foley run. He was known to make stops along the way to bring needed supplies to residents. He was reputed to have been one of the engineers who would stop the train for an hour or so and let the passengers pick dewberries along the tracks. He is pictured in front of one of the last passenger cars. (Courtesy of Foley Museum.)

16

THE L&N BAND. The L&N Railroad was one of the largest employers on the Gulf Coast. A formal photograph of the employee band was taken in Mobile at the main switchyard there. Even though passenger service was discontinued in 1950, the Foley yard remained active until 1975, at which time the tracks were removed. Former employees and other rail enthusiasts have created a museum located in the old depot. (Courtesy of Foley Museum.)

CIRCUIT-RIDING PREACHER. Many religious leaders who served in the Foley area were itinerant or circuit-riding ministers. Pictured above is Rev. E.A. Wendland riding his buggy pulled by his chestnut horse Davey. He traveled to several communities in south Baldwin County to serve the newly founded Lutheran churches from about 1911 to 1920. (Courtesy of St. Paul's Lutheran Church.)

ST. MARGARET'S CATHOLIC CHURCH. John Foley donated land to any bona fide religious group for a church. Under the tenure of Fr. Adam Heibel, the first Catholic church was built on an acre lot on the west edge of town in 1911. It was knocked from its foundations in the 1916 hurricane but was replaced and braced. A cemetery was designated on the property, and the wooden crucifix carved by Matthew Sute was the centerpiece of the cemetery. Sute also built the parish hall in 1918. (Photograph by Penny H. Taylor.)

ST. PAUL'S LUTHERAN CHURCH. Founding members William Stelk, Fred Brockman, Henry Brockman, and William Doege organized St. Paul's Church in April 1912. The first church building, pictured above, was completed in 1913 on lots donated by the Magnolia Springs Land Company. Fred Brockman did much of the work. (Courtesy of St. Paul's Lutheran Church.)

BAPTIST CHURCH. Attendees at a nail service were photographed here in front of the Baptist church on February 10, 1910. The pastor of the church was Rev. D.H. Daffin at the time. The nail service was the concluding event of the revival week conducted by visiting evangelist W.E. Lockler. (Courtesy of Foley Museum.)

METHODIST CHURCH. First begun as a union Sunday school, the Grace Methodist Episcopal Church was built on lots on the intersection of Laurel Avenue and Pine Street in 1908. Another Methodist church was organized in 1925 and met in the school auditorium. The two churches joined in 1945 and worshipped in the church building on Pine Street and Laurel Avenue. A new brick building was completed in 1951 and is still standing but owned by the school system. A new church was built to the north in 1961. (Courtesy of Foley Museum.)

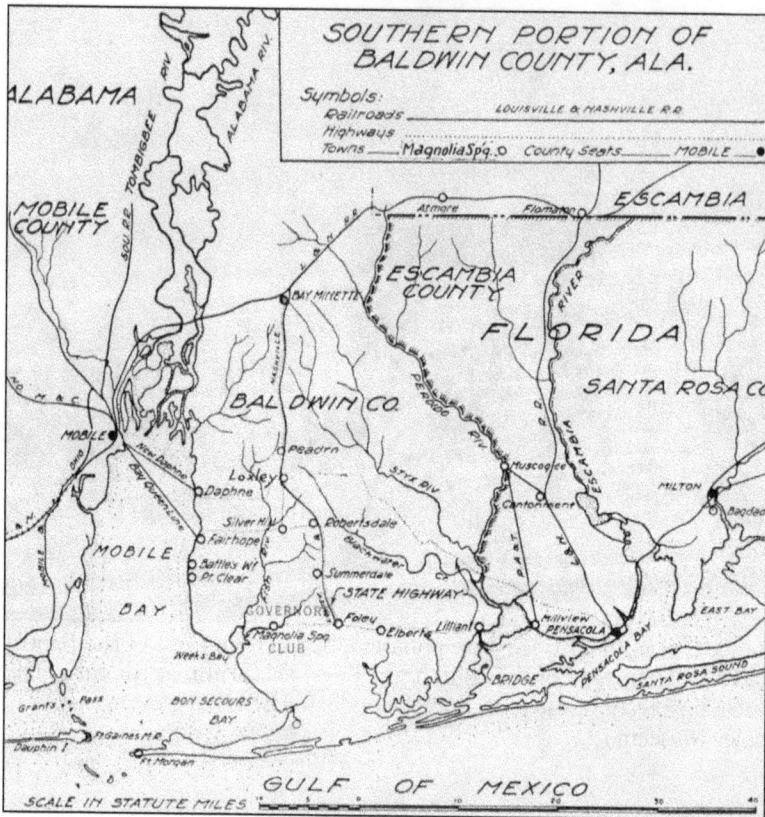

EARLY MAP. As shown in this early map of Baldwin County, the only roads in the southern part of the county ran from Magnolia Springs to Miflin. These were the primary points of landing for riverboats bringing supplies to the settlers. The rail line, as pictured, began to open up the farmland in the area by providing transportation for the produce grown on the farms. (Courtesy of Weeks Bay National Estuarine Research Reserve.)

LITTLE CHICAGO. In one of Walter Anderson's cartoon inserts, Foley was featured as being known as "Little Chicago." Not only did the founder J.B. Foley hail from Chicago, but many of the new farmers also migrated from the Midwest. (Courtesy of Baldwin County Department of Archives and History.)

Two

FARMS AND FORESTS

COUNTRY SCHOOLHOUSE. One-room schoolhouses were built three to four miles apart. The county paid the teacher's salary, but the community boarded the teacher and provided all school supplies. This school was located at Caney Branch, a community near Elberta. When the towns built larger schools, most one-room schools were consolidated, and the children moved to the town schools. (Courtesy of Harriet Brill Outlaw.)

ORANGE GROVE IN MAGNOLIA SPRINGS. The photograph above was used in advertisements throughout the Midwest. The tree is representative of orange trees in the grove of Dr. Frank Winberg, who had a farm about 10 miles north of Magnolia Springs. In the 1923 season, his yield was over 200 boxes per acre. (Courtesy of Foley Museum.)

PLANTING CITRUS TREES. By 1915, there were 424,576 satsuma orange trees and 34,285 grapefruit trees planted in orchards in the county. Satsumas were selling for 45¢ a dozen. During the hurricane of 1916, most other crops were ruined, but the satsuma trees weathered the storm fairly well, and the crop yield that year was successful. (Courtesy of Foley Museum.)

KRISCHER MULES. Mules, such as the two pictured above, were necessary commodities on family farms where every member had chores to do. Mules Jim and Jack are pictured here with, from left to right, Anna, Bill, John, and Andy Krischer on their farm near Elberta. (Courtesy of Baldwin County Heritage Museum.)

BOUNTIFUL FRUIT. Satsumas, first introduced in America by a Japanese native, were more flavorful and resistant to frost than oranges. Dr. W.H. Ludwig of Rock Island, Illinois, planted more than 2,000 trees in 1910 and, by 1913, was harvesting 1,200 crates. Workers wore regulation gloves and used specially designed nippers to harvest the fruit. (Courtesy of Weeks Bay National Estuarine Research Reserve.)

DIGGING UP SWEETS. In a letter from Wilson Corey written home to Anderson, Indiana, he proclaims the bountiful resources conducive to farming. He reports that the soil is red sandy loam and red clay subsoil with no clods or rocks. He says that the principal crop is sweet potatoes, grown by hundreds and thousands. He also mentions that a man needs only half as much land to farm since two crops per year can be planted—potatoes in the spring and wheat in the summer and fall. (Courtesy of Foley Museum.)

HAULING POTATOES TO TOWN. School was dismissed about the time that the potato harvest came in. The entire community worked to dig, sort, bag, or haul the produce to market. Most potatoes were shipped on the rail line, as trucks did not have the capacity to handle the large quantities. Here is pictured the line of loaded wagons waiting to be weighed and sold to the brokers at the potato sheds, where the potatoes were graded and packaged. The depot is on the left. (Courtesy of Foley Museum.)

LINED UP AT POTATO SHEDS. During the heyday of potato marketing, farmers planted and sold the Bliss Triumph variety, which was an 85-day crop. They could be harvested and marketed during the time that the Dakota potatoes in storage were starting to ruin because of sprouting and the Florida crops were dying off. During the peak years in the 1950s, more than 40,000 acres were planted in potatoes in the county. (Courtesy of Foley Museum.)

TRUCK-FARMING PRODUCE. Every local family raised and preserved vegetables for consumption during the year. There were also many cash crops that performed well. Cucumbers were among the most profitable, as they have a long bearing season. Corn, melons, peanuts, soybeans, and cotton were also among the top-producing cash crops. Pictured here, farmers are inspecting the large heads of cabbage grown near Elberta. (Courtesy of Foley Museum.)

MULES FOR WORK. William Schenk is pictured with the beloved mules Jim and Jack, who belonged to Fred Tabert. William was a faithful employee at the Tabert farm on Kleinschmidt Road in Elberta. Mules were a part of the daily farm life for many years, providing the power for plowing and cultivating. (Courtesy of Baldwin County Heritage Museum.)

TRACTORS ARRIVING AT THE FARM. The postcard above was mailed to Fred Koehler in Mobile from his brother Edgar in Elberta. The message reads, "Swft P.C., Alabama, July 17, 1910. Dear Brother, I will write a few lines. We are all well. Hope you the same. We are having plenty of rain here now. It is good weather for the crops to grow. That picture on the other side is me with the 20 horse power engine. I will write a letter soon. Best regards and love from Edgar K." (Courtesy of June Taylor.)

FLOWER INDUSTRY.
Growing long-stemmed gladioli, or "sword lilies," was a major industry for more than 40 years. By 1939, several companies were growing and shipping the flowers, and production was so bountiful at peak times that extra night trains were run to ship the flowers by Railway Express. Pictured at right is an unidentified man on the left assisting owner Jack Van Lierop, working at the Van Lierop Shipping plant. (Courtesy of Foley Museum.)

COOPERATIVE ASSOCIATION. Local farmers, who built the facility pictured here, established the Farmers' Mutual Cooperative Association in 1918. H.M. Hamburg came to work here in 1935 and, in 1949, became the owner; the business was named H.M. Hamburg and Sons, Inc. Farmers obtaining seeds and fertilizer from the cooperative signed agreements mortgaging such items as their mules, tractors, homes, and so on. (Courtesy of Foley Museum.)

CORRALLING CATTLE FOR MARKET. Until the "stock laws" were enacted in 1948, cattle ranged free in the woods. When sold, they were rounded up by whip-wielding men called "crackers," herded to the local depot, and loaded on boxcars for shipping to slaughterhouses in the North and Midwest. These cattle were Pineywoods cattle, commonly called the firecracker breed. They were not dehorned to prevent infection common with that process. (Courtesy of Foley Museum.)

DIPPING VAT. In the early 1900s, Alabama initiated an aggressive attack on Texas fever, carried by ticks. County governments were required to build vats and assure that all cattle were driven through the arsenic solution. The one pictured above was south of Elberta on Miflin Road and was built around 1925. Many farmers felt that this requirement overstepped their rights, and some vats were destroyed by dynamite. (Courtesy of June Taylor.)

HAULING LOGS TO MILL. The leading economic industry in Baldwin County until the 21st century was lumber and naval stores production. Longleaf pine trees were cut in the forests and hauled by wagons pulled by oxen to nearby streams, where they were floated to the sawmills. (Courtesy of Weeks Bay National Estuarine Research Reserve.)

MILLING LUMBER. The sawmill owned by Charles and Ira Swift pictured above was only one of the mills owned by Swift Lumber Company. Located on waterways, the mills were the destination of the logs harvested in nearby forests. The milled lumber was then loaded on barges and shipped to Mobile for worldwide distribution, primarily Brazil. The invention of steam lumber mills greatly increased the production. (Courtesy of Swift-Coles Historic Home.)

HAULING PINE RESIN TO THE STILL. The production of naval stores, or turpentine and rosin, was a primary industry in the gulf area. The products were critical in the shipbuilding industry; rosin was used to waterproof the hulls, while turpentine was used in the paints. Resin was gathered from pine trees and hauled in the barrels to the distilleries, or "stills," located throughout the county. (Courtesy of Weeks Bay National Estuarine Research Reserve.)

LOADING THE BARRELS. Pinesap, weeping from the trees through slashes made through the bark of the tree, was collected in clay or metal cups placed below slashes. Chips were made in mature pine trees at least nine inches in diameter in the spring of the year. Once a month, the sap was collected in barrels and hauled to local stills. (Courtesy of Weeks Bay National Estuarine Research Reserve.)

30

CATFACE MARKINGS. Each spring, a V-shaped slash was made above the slash of the previous year. As the slashes were added each year, the appearance of the scarred trees was known as a "catface." A tree was productive for 10 to 15 years. Very large trees of more than 14 inches in diameter could be chipped on two sides, increasing the production of sap from the tree. (Courtesy of Weeks Bay National Estuarine Research Reserve.)

BARRELS FOR SHIPPING. Pinesap was boiled under pressure at the distilleries. Eight to ten barrels of sap were needed to do one run of the boiler and produced six barrels of rosin and two barrels of turpentine. Pictured here is the A.M. Moses Company loading dock. Barrels such as these were destroyed in 1865 in Magnolia Springs to prevent capture by Union forces in Baldwin County. (Courtesy of Weeks Bay National Estuarine Research Reserve.)

4-H OAK TREE

THE FIRST CORN GROWN BY WHITE MEN ON THE GULF COAST WAS PLANTED ON DAUPHIN ISLAND IN THE YEAR 1702.

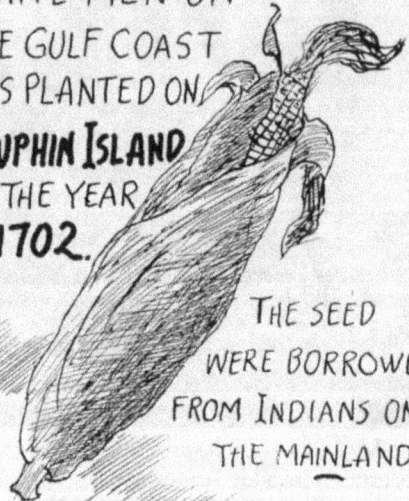

A SECTION OF OAK ROOTS FOUND BY HARVEY UNDERWOOD ON HIS FARM NEAR FOLEY, ALA., HAD GROWN FIRMLY TOGETHER TO MAKE THE 4-H SYMBOL.

THE SEED WERE BORROWED FROM INDIANS ON THE MAINLAND.

THE FIRST "KITCHEN UTENSILS" MADE AND USED IN THE SOUTHLAND WERE MADE FROM GOURDS, TREATED WITH SCALDING WATER AND SCRAPED, INSIDE, TO MAKE A HARDENED SURFACE.

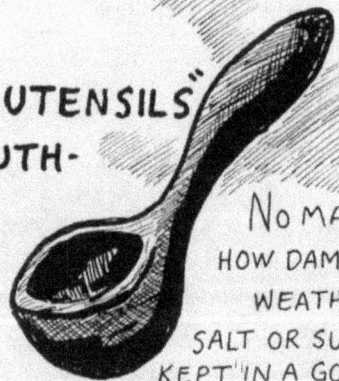

NO MATTER HOW DAMP THE WEATHER, SALT OR SUGAR KEPT IN A GOURD WILL ALWAYS STAY DRY. W.O.

THEY WERE USED BEFORE POTTERY, AND THEY ARE STILL BEING USED TODAY.

A "SOUTHLAND" SKETCH. Harvey Underwood supplied the information for this article. The Underwoods farmed many acres north and west of Foley. They provided a school for their community, which was known both as Yupon and as Underwood. (Courtesy of Baldwin County Department of Archives and History.)

Three

FOLEY MOVES FORWARD

NEW MODERN SCHOOLHOUSE. After the first schoolhouse was badly damaged by the hurricane of 1916, Dr. Sibley Holmes wrote to John B. Foley to request land for a new school. The school system could only fund wooden structures at the time, and so local businessmen contributed funds and mortgaged the land to build the first brick schoolhouse in Baldwin County. The building to the right was added about five years later. (Courtesy of Foley Museum.)

REAL ESTATE AGENTS. Claude Peteet was one of the earliest real estate agents in Foley, and the building pictured above may well be the oldest building still standing in Foley. Closed when Claude Peteet died in 1961, the building remained locked and its contents safe until it was restored in 2011. News articles referred to it as a time capsule of Foley history. (Courtesy of Foley Museum.)

CROSBY'S DRUGSTORE. The first brick building on the corner of McKenzie and Laurel Streets was the Drietz building, in which Crosby's Drugstore was located upstairs near Dr. Sibley Holmes's practice. When Drietz expanded the building, Crosby's moved downstairs and the doctor's offices were expanded upstairs, later becoming the Holmes Memorial Hospital. (Courtesy of Foley Museum.)

CHILDRESS MARKET. One of the grocery stores in Foley was Childress, which was first located on McKenzie Street next to the Wee Bite Café. It moved to this brick building on the north side of Laurel Avenue. (Courtesy of Foley Museum.)

DIXIE FURNITURE. Dixie Furniture Company occupied the building on East Laurel Avenue that was formerly Wenzel's Store. The upstairs housed a dance floor at one time run by Howard Davis. When Bob Young, who also owned the Dixie Hotel in Fairhope, purchased the building and opened Dixie Furniture Company, he added the west section. Eventually, the two-story original store was demolished. (Courtesy of Foley Museum.)

HOLK DEPARTMENT STORE. George Holk built his general store, pictured above at the top center of the photograph, on the southeast corner of Laurel Avenue and McKenzie Street in 1921. His family lived upstairs, where two of their eight children were born. The family later moved to a home on North McKenzie Street. George Holk was mayor from 1924 to 1926, and his son Arthur was mayor from 1976 to 1996. Hotel Magnolia is pictured at the bottom of the photograph. (Courtesy of Foley Museum.)

FOLEY BAKERY. The Foley Bakery, owned by the Hartman family and found in the corner of this building, was well known for its incredible baked goods as well as its hamburgers, handmade by Kenny Franklin. Students in the 1950s could leave the high school campus for lunch. Many would jaunt the few blocks to the bakery, eat lunch, and return to school before the tardy bell rang. (Courtesy of Foley Museum.)

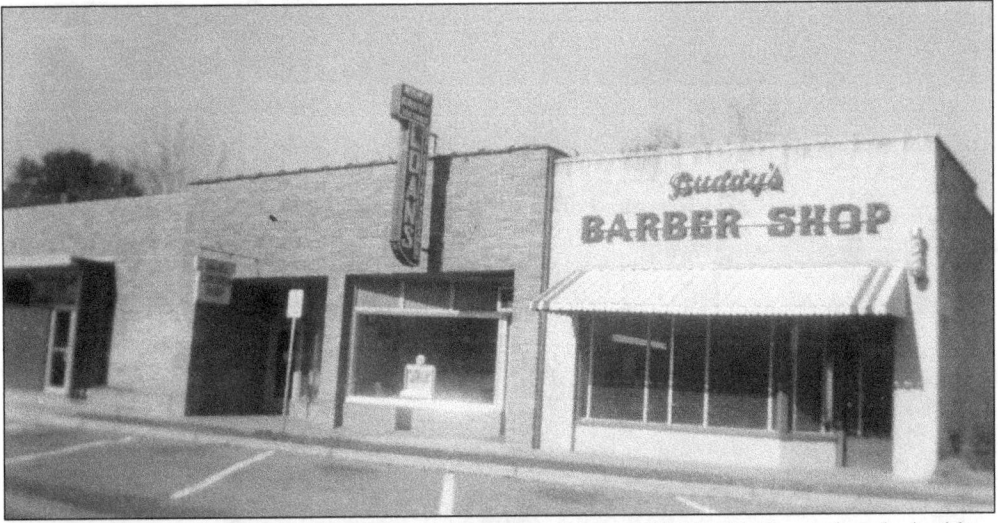

STOREFRONT ROW. Buddy's Barber Shop was owned and operated by Buddy Pierce, but the building was first built to house Fred Walker Plumbing. Cliff Beck ran the loan institution next door, and the end business was Parker and Woods Accounting. Ebert Agency moved into the building in the 1950s. (Courtesy of Foley Museum.)

MASONIC HALL. The Masons laid the cornerstone for their Masonic hall in 1926, complete with a time capsule. From the 1940s through the 1960s, the downstairs was opened as a youth center that held weekend dances. The upstairs remained the temple, where not only the Masons met but also the auxiliary Masonic organizations—Eastern Star, DeMolay, and Rainbow Girls. The water tower in the photograph was built in 1928, when the city water system was initiated. (Courtesy of Foley Museum.)

NATIONAL GUARD ARMORY. The armory pictured above was built in 1936, but its 106th Motorcycle Company, 31st Division, had been established in the 1920s. Fifty of those National Guardsmen were called to duty in 1940. The unit had 16 Indian bikes left over from World War I. After World War II, the unit became Company G, 200th Infantry Regiment, 31st Division, and was called to active duty for the Korean War. (Courtesy of Foley Museum.)

STACEY'S DRUGSTORE. The grand Foley Hotel was built on the corner of Alston Street and Laurel Avenue in 1928. The corner was occupied by first by Dumas Drugs and later by Bob Stacey, who ran the pharmacy in the building. It is still know locally as the "Old Tyme Drugstore" with its original marble counter, fountain drinks, and a jukebox. (Courtesy of Foley Museum.)

THREE GENERATIONS OF EBERTS. John Frederick Ebert moved to Foley in 1904 with his wife, Anna, and their two-year-old son, Charles John Ebert. Pictured here from left to right are John Frederick, Charles John Jr., and Charles John Ebert, three generations in 1930 at the home place west of Foley. The Ebert Agency was started by Charles John and has been in the family for three generations and more than 80 years. (Courtesy of Charles Ebert.)

FOLEY AS A TOWN. On January 8, 1915, the citizens of Foley voted in favor of incorporation with a vote of 21 to 6. The vote provided for a mayor and five councilmen to be elected, and G.I. Weatherly won the February ballot. Councilmen were Henry Brockman, Charles Boller, Patrick Cooney, John Lehr, and W. Stelk. Weatherly served only until he resigned in October and was replaced by C.C. Boller. (Courtesy of Foley Museum.)

Dr. Sibley Holmes. The Sibley Holmes Memorial Hospital, located in the second story of the brick building on the corner of McKenzie Street and Laurel Avenue, was operated from 1936 through 1958 by Dr. W.C. Holmes, who named the hospital for his father, Sibley. Sibley Holmes was an Alabama senator and mayor of Foley from 1930 to 1933 and had practiced medicine in the same location. (Courtesy of Homes Medical Museum.)

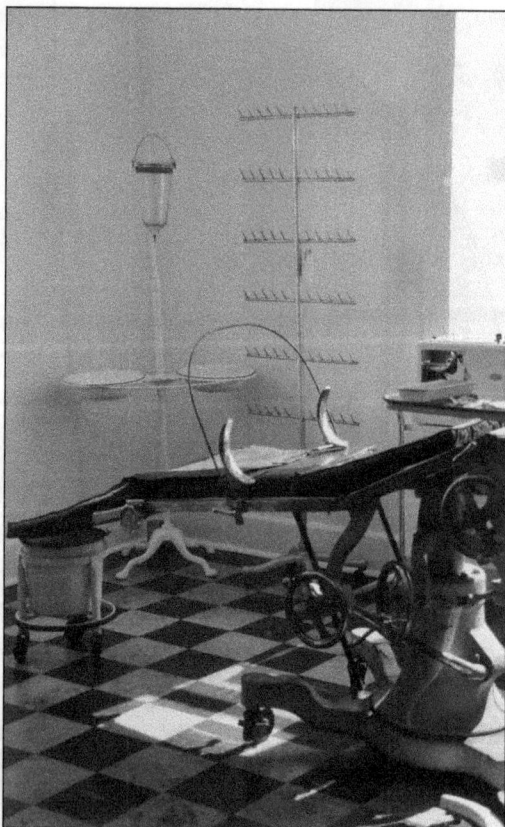

Hospital Room. W.C. Holmes and his wife, Philomene, a registered nurse, operated the hospital for 23 years. While Dr. Holmes was serving in World War II, Philomene kept the doors opened. The hospital had patient rooms, examination rooms, offices, a kitchen, and a waiting room. Dr. Holmes conducted routine treatments of patients but referred surgeries to specialists who came from Mobile. (Photograph by Penny H. Taylor.)

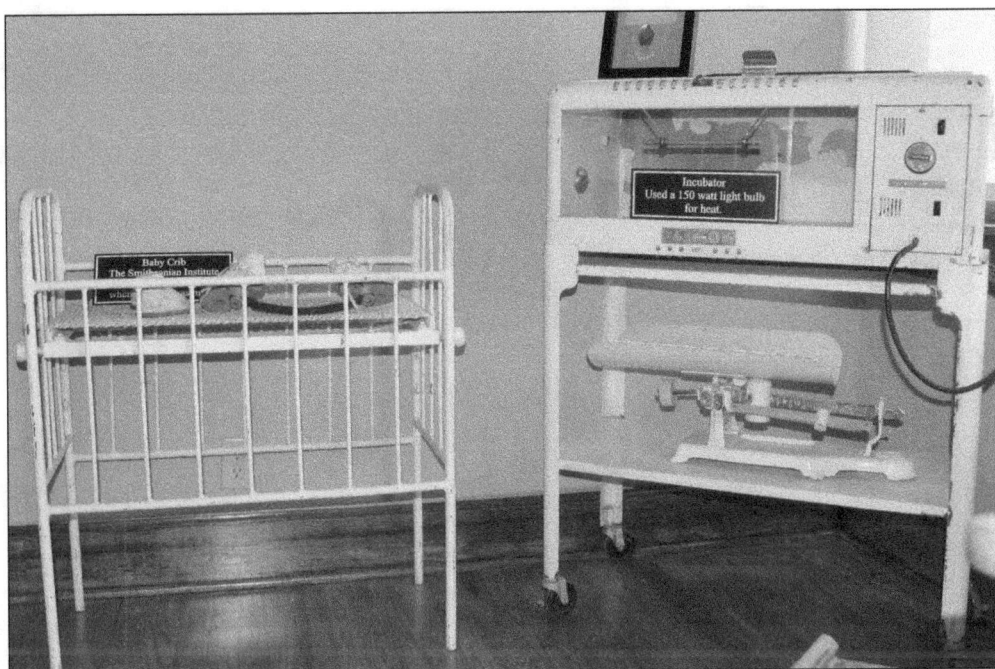

HOLMES'S BABIES. More than 300 babies were delivered by W.C. and/or his wife, Philomene, and have been dubbed "Holmes Babies." Babies were delivered at homes as well as in the hospital. Pictured above are a crib and an incubator used for babies needing special care. The hospital is preserved today as the Holmes Medical Museum and houses many of the original instruments used in treating patients. (Photograph by Penny H. Taylor.)

COOK'S MARKET. The grocery store owned and operated by the Cook family was located beneath the Holmes Hospital. It was the first store in Foley with a butcher, two of whom are pictured on the left of the 1935 photograph above. On the right are Claude Glenn Cook and his son, Joseph Earl. Joseph later was awarded a Distinguished Service Medal during World War II. (Courtesy of Gail Cook Colvert.)

STANDARD OIL. Several oil companies sprang up to meet the needs of growing numbers of automobiles and tractors. The Texaco distributorship was run by the Boller family, and Meder Motors was selling Model T sedans for $625 in 1922. Charles Ebert developed the Standard Oil service station pictured above on the corner of Rose Avenue and McKenzie Street. (Courtesy of Foley Museum.)

SOUTHERN FOUNDRIES. One of the most successful enterprises in Foley was Southern Foundries. Pictured above is the mill in its first year of operation in the early 1960s. Pictured from left to right are David Chapman, Butch Woodyard, Shortie Shoots, and Willie Shoots. (Courtesy of Foley Museum.)

42

FOLEY THEATER. Besides the Two Torches located in the Foley Hotel Building, there was the Foley Theater on Alston Street, owned by the Tisdale family. The photograph above was for the controversial showing of *Mom and Dad*, which had separate show times for male and female patrons. The Troyer Building shown to the left was the former Dumas Drugs, and after a stucco exterior was added, it was the Troyer Funeral Home. (Courtesy of Foley Museum.)

WEE BITE CAFÉ. The first on the left of these buildings facing east on McKenzie Street was the office of R.C. Clark. The Wee Bite Café was formerly M&F Store, run by Max Davis. After M&F moved, Ross Woodall opened the Wee Bite Café, which was later owned by Lydia and J.W. Andress. Childress Market is to the right, and the last store was the John Deere dealership run by Max Lawrenz. (Courtesy of Foley Museum.)

POLICE DEPARTMENT. By the 1940s, the city had a police force led by B.D. Cobb, who served as chief for more than 30 years. Pictured above are, from left to right, (first row) unidentified, Wilbur Albers, unidentified, Chief B.D. Cobb, Frank Osborn, and Ray Morrison; (second row) Ham Hall, Judge Honecc, ? Steadman, unidentified, and Van Iderstine, chief of police in Daphne. (Courtesy of Foley Museum.)

SESQUICENTENNIAL CELEBRATION. Towns throughout Baldwin County participated in activities celebrating the 150th anniversary of the county. Pictured are James Hawkins (left) and Guy McAlily (far right); they have jailed Chan Smith (left) and Max Lawrenz (right), who are waiting to make bail. Citizens in costume boarded a train in Foley and made the round trip to Bay Minette for the last time a passenger train ran on the tracks. (Courtesy of Foley Museum.)

AARONVILLE SCHOOL. The community of Aaronville was home to many families of African American descent who had migrated to Foley for work in the turpentine stills, railroad, or agriculture industries. They built a one-room school that served children in grades one through seven. A new school was built in Aaronville in 1960 to provide high school education. The school closed in 1970, when it was consolidated during the integration movement. The building became the Foley Middle School. Pictured here are children performing during the annual event known as Shakuntala. (Both, courtesy of Foley Library.)

SCHOOL YEARBOOK STAFF. During the years Aaronville School operated as a high school, the annuals were produced by the students. Pictured are, from left to right, (sitting) Fannie Armstrong, Sarah Porter, George Johnson, Carolyn Rodgers, Shirley Heard, and Corinne Robertson; (standing) Donald Jones, Esaw Hackett, Samuel Franklin, Carol McCall, and Shirley Watkins (inset). (Courtesy of Foley Library.)

DEMOLITION OF TWO-STORY SCHOOLHOUSE. The 1916 two-story schoolhouse was first Foley High School. After the construction of the new school in 1921, the two-story building was the elementary school. Originally, the school had an auditorium upstairs and was designated as the first agricultural school in Baldwin County using the Smith Act funds for vocational and agricultural programs. It was demolished in 1959 to make way for the new library for the high school. (Courtesy of Foley Museum.)

NEW HIGH SCHOOL AUDITORIUM. Soon after the school opened in 1921, a full-size auditorium was constructed by the county school system. At this time, the only high schools in the county were Foley, Fairhope, Bay Minette, and Robertsdale, each with an auditorium that served many functions in the community. (Courtesy of Baldwin County Historical Development Commission.)

TELEPHONE COMPANY. The first telephone company in Foley, South Baldwin Telephone Company, was organized in 1908 and managed by J.L. Crouch. In 1914, C.A. Boller became manager, and in 1916, Frank Walker, who acquired the Loxley and Silverhill exchanges, reorganized it. It was sold to Ward Snook of Ohio and renamed the Gulf Telephone Company in the mid-1930s, and a new office on Laurel Avenue was constructed. Ward's son John became president of the company and a leading citizen in Foley. (Courtesy of Jeannie Collins.)

SOUTHLAND SKETCHES

by Walter Overton

SHOWN HERE ARE THE REMAINS OF A BAKERY OVEN CONSTRUCTED AT JOSEPHINE, ALA., BY MR. J. TAGSHERER IN 1914.

AFTER THE MANNER OF "HANDCRAFTED" BREAD, THE LOAVES WERE PLACED IN THE OVEN AFTER EVERY TRACE OF THE FIRE HAD BEEN REMOVED. THE HEAT RETAINED BY THE SPECIAL BRICKS SLOW-BAKED THEM TO A DELICIOUS CRUST AND TEXTURE NOT OBTAINABLE EVEN IN HOMEMADE BREAD.

A NUMBER OF PERDIDO BAY SETTLEMENTS WERE SUPPLIED REGULARLY FROM THIS OVEN BY MR. TAGSHERER, WHO HAD LEARNED HIS CRAFT AS AN APPRENTICE IN THE "OLD COUNTRY" WHILE STILL A BOY.

A CAREFUL VIGIL WAS MAINTAINED WHILE BREAD WAS IN THE OVEN TO MAKE SURE THAT ALL WENT WELL AND THE LOAVES WERE REMOVED AT EXACTLY THE RIGHT MOMENT.

LATER ON, THE BAKERY WAS MOVED TO FOLEY, AND PEOPLE ALL ALONG THE L and N IN SOUTH BALDWIN COUNTY ENJOYED BREAD BETTER THAN "MOTHER USED TO MAKE."

J.O. SCHOFNER, FARMING IN MOBILE COUNTY, PRODUCED 13,000 GALLONS OF CANE SYRUP ON A 10-ACRE FARM.

PURE CANE SYRUP

TWO MAGNOLIA TREES, GROWING AT HEALING SPRINGS, ALA., JOINED FORCES TO FORM THE LETTER "N".

A LIMB FROM ONE TREE CROSSED OVER TO GROW INTO THE OTHER TREE, 25 FEET AWAY. DRAWN FROM A SKETCH SENT TO SOUTHLAND SKETCHES BY MRS. J.A. FREEMAN, OF SELMA, TO WHOM, MANY THANKS. W.O.

HERITAGE OF BAKING. The Tagsherer Bakery in Foley had its beginnings in Josephine. This "Southland Sketch" by Walter Overton featured the brick ovens built in 1914 east of Foley on Perdido Bay. J. Tagsherer had learned the process of baking bread in brick ovens at his home in the old country while still a boy. He built the ovens to replicate the process. His business supplied bread to most of the residents in south Baldwin County. (Courtesy of Baldwin County Department of Archives and History.)

Four

ELBERTA

FIRST ELBERTA SCHOOL. Education in the town of Elberta had its beginning in seven one-room schools built by the Baldwin County Colonization Company scattered over the district about every three to four miles. The Elberta School pictured here was built in 1904 on Main Street in the newly formed colony. (Courtesy of Baldwin County Heritage Museum.)

EARLY ELBERTA SETTLEMENT. In 1903, a group of businessmen organized the Baldwin County Colonization Company under Alabama law and purchased about 55,000 acres of land in southeast Baldwin County. Some of the earliest buildings are pictured above. From left to right are Hague's Store, Schroeder Store and the post office, the Ohls home, and Loewen Store. The Lindoerfer Store is in the foreground. (Courtesy of June Taylor.)

STREET SCENE. The company first cleared 20 acres for the town and built 10 miles of roads along section lines. It offered 20- and 40-acre parcels, all facing roads. The earliest buildings include the Hotel Elberta, pictured in the center of the photograph. Also pictured are, from left to right, Loewen Store and Lindoerfer Store. St. Mark's Church is to the right in the background. (Courtesy of June Taylor.)

FRED OHLS HOME. First built as the Colony Company Hotel, Piney Grove Hotel still stands at Main and Olive Streets. It was built in 1904, when only 12 families lived in Elberta. However, most of the workmen bought 40 acres of land and stayed. The first manager of the hotel, Gustav Koch, is acknowledged as the first permanent settler. It was later owned and operated by the Fred Ohls family. (Courtesy of June Taylor.)

ELBERTA'S SECOND HOTEL. The hotel pictured here was built by Pierre Lamont, who soon sold it to Philip Ickler, an agent of the Baldwin County Colonization Company. It was a large white wooden structure and became the social center of the town. Memories of a 1920 grand Christmas Eve dance with a 10-foot tree bedecked with 200 wax tapers are recorded in early memoirs of residents. Ickler later dismantled the hotel and moved it to Lillian. (Courtesy of Baldwin County Heritage Museum.)

BRETZ HOTEL. In 1920–1921, the Elberta Ranch Hotel was built on Highway 98 at Alabama Street. More familiarly known as the Bretz Hotel, it was operated by the Adam Bretz family until they sold it to J.A. Pilgrim. In the early years, many schoolteachers lived there, and later the Pilgrims renovated the building to house Navy personnel stationed at nearby Barin Field. The hotel was razed in 1965. (Courtesy of Baldwin County Heritage Museum.)

BRETZ FAMILY. Adam Bretz and his family were among the earliest permanent residents of Elberta. In the hotel, Adam Bretz had installed a beautiful wood dance floor of two-toned tongue-in-groove pine boards, and Babette Bretz was known for her wonderful culinary skills. Sunday dinners were served for 50¢ every week to a packed dining room. Also pictured is their daughter Gertrude. (Courtesy of Baldwin County Heritage Museum.)

KOEHLER HOUSE AND POST OFFICE. The first post office for Elberta was located at Swift Mill, three miles from town, but an Elberta office was established in Schroeder's Store in 1906, and Joseph Lechner was the first postmaster. After a new post office was built by Adam Frank, Postmistress Anna Kenney (pictured) and her two sons, Harold and Clarence, lived in the building from 1913 to 1933. (Courtesy of Baldwin County Heritage Museum.)

ISAAC LOEWEN STORE. L.A. Rinke of Chicago first operated his store in the Elberta Hotel while his two-story building was being constructed on the southwest corner of the main streets in town. The general store carried clothing, food, supplies, farm equipment, and animal feed. (Courtesy of Baldwin County Heritage Museum.)

VOGELGESANG RESIDENCE. These images are of a 1911 postcard mailed to Louis Ludeking in Newark, New Jersey, from his brother Henry. E.A. Vogelgesang, who was one of the early managers of the Pine Grove Hotel, and he and his family were among the earliest permanent residents. Later, the Doege family lived in the house, which is on the corner of US Highway 98 and Alabama Street. The message on the postcard is written in German, as German was the primary language of Elberta residents until the last half of the 20th century. There were more than 60 dialects and languages in the town at the early stages of settlement. (Both, courtesy of June Taylor.)

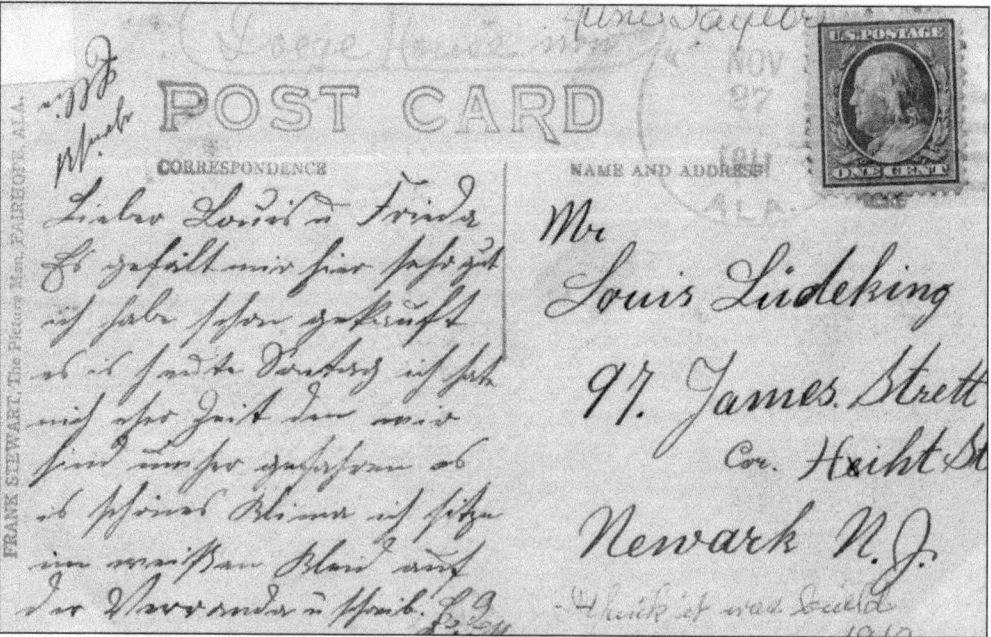

FARMERS HALL. The Elberta Farmers Club was organized in 1908 and met monthly in a building the group constructed on the corner of Alabama and Pine Streets. They discussed agriculture methods and established marketing plans for the local farmers. The building was dedicated on July 4, 1916, with a *Weinlesserfest*, or "grape festival." The photograph above shows a group gathered for a picnic party. (Courtesy of Baldwin County Heritage Museum.)

FARMERS HALL DRAMA. A group of dramatists performed many plays for school and civic benefits. They became well known and even performed in the Saenger Theater in Pensacola. Pictured here are, from left to right, (first row) Lydia Collier, Mabel Lenz, Edna Noltensmeier, Bill Haupt, and Sudye Garrett; (second row) N.P. Christensen, Alfred Neuman, Henry Gebert, John Schnatz, and Bonnie Keltz. (Courtesy of Baldwin County Heritage Museum.)

MUSIC IN ELBERTA. The local dance band pictured above was one of many that played for gatherings at the Farmers Hall. Pictured are, from left to right, Irma Ulrich, Toney Scheer, Steve Scheer, and Gus Lovitz. A group of men who loved singing formed the Gesang Verein, or the Elberta Glee Club, which practiced every Tuesday night in the hall. The 1938 members are, from left to right, (first row) Paul Haupt, William Konrad, John Schnatz, Adolph Ebentheuer, Walter Salzmann, and Ludwig Lindoerfer; (second row) August Collier, Steven Vogel, Karl Nachtigall, Herman Ulbricht, Alfred Neumann, Edward Erdman, Paul Warzacha, and Louis Bretz; (third row) Alfred Riebe, John Reiner, Samuel DePaola, Adam Bretz, Emil Ritty, Herman Lawrenz, Jacob Krischer, and Fred Siebert; (fourth row) Mathew Neumann, Sebastian Bitto, Joseph Braxmeier, Adolph Perske, Henry Gebert, Herman Rummel, and Paul Traumer. (Above, courtesy of June Taylor; below, courtesy of Baldwin County Heritage Museum.)

MUSICALE EXTRAVAGANZA. These girls performed a musical, which was supervised by Ella Starnagle. Pictured from left to right are (first row) Anna Berg, Elsie Brenner, Elizabeth Neumann, Helen Lenz, unidentified, Wilma Schwab, Loretta Schreck, and Bonnie Keltz; (second row) Catherine Neumann, unidentified, Sylvia Bartz, Martha Haupt, Margaret Lawrenz, and Erna Hinkelman. (Courtesy of Baldwin County Heritage Museum.)

KOEHLER FAMILY. Herman Koehler and his wife, Frieda, were born in Germany, immigrated to Nebraska, and then settled in Elberta in 1908. They were ardent supporters of Elberta and often hosted interested home-seekers in their house in town. Here, the family is celebrating the Fourth of July and enjoying homegrown watermelons. Pictured are, from left to right, (sitting) Herman (top) and Henry (bottom); (standing) Elizabeth, Charles, Hulda, Erwin, Herman, and Frieda. (Courtesy of Baldwin County Heritage Museum.)

COMING TO TOWN. The Ebentheuer family poses for a 1926 photograph in front of the Collier Theater, which was located to the left of the photograph. The camera is facing east on Highway 98. The Ludeking family moved to north Elberta from New Jersey in 1912. Daughter Elsie married Adolf Ebentheuer in 1918. They lived on Miflin Road. Pictured are, from left to right, Dorothy, Elsie, Henry, and Ella Ebentheuer. Elsie is the grandmother of local historian June Taylor. (Courtesy of June Taylor.)

LEX THEATER. Lex Theater, pictured here, was built by J.A. Pilgrim, who had purchased the Bretz Hotel next door. Two small shops flanked the entrance. One was Emily's Sweet Shoppe, run by Emily Pfaff, and the other was the Elberta Variety Shop, owned by Robert Hartley. (Courtesy of Baldwin County Heritage Museum.)

RIDE TO SCHOOL. Joe Salzmann was born in1926 to parents who had moved to Elberta from Switzerland. He is pictured on the pony he rode to school at St. Benedict's for grades one through eight. After-school chores included bringing in the cattle, which were free-range at that time. He graduated from Foley in 1944, joined the Navy, and returned to Elberta, where he served as a rural route mail carrier. He is pictured with his father, Walter. (Courtesy of Baldwin County Heritage Museum.)

PROUD WORKMEN. The era following World War I brought another building boom to Elberta. These builders—from left to right, Joseph Leginstein, Charlie Hagendorfer, and Fred Hagendorfer— are constructing a home behind Pluscht Store in 1926. Manufacturers of bricks formed from cement were scattered throughout the county and supplied the building material of choice in the 1920s. (Courtesy of Baldwin County Heritage Museum.)

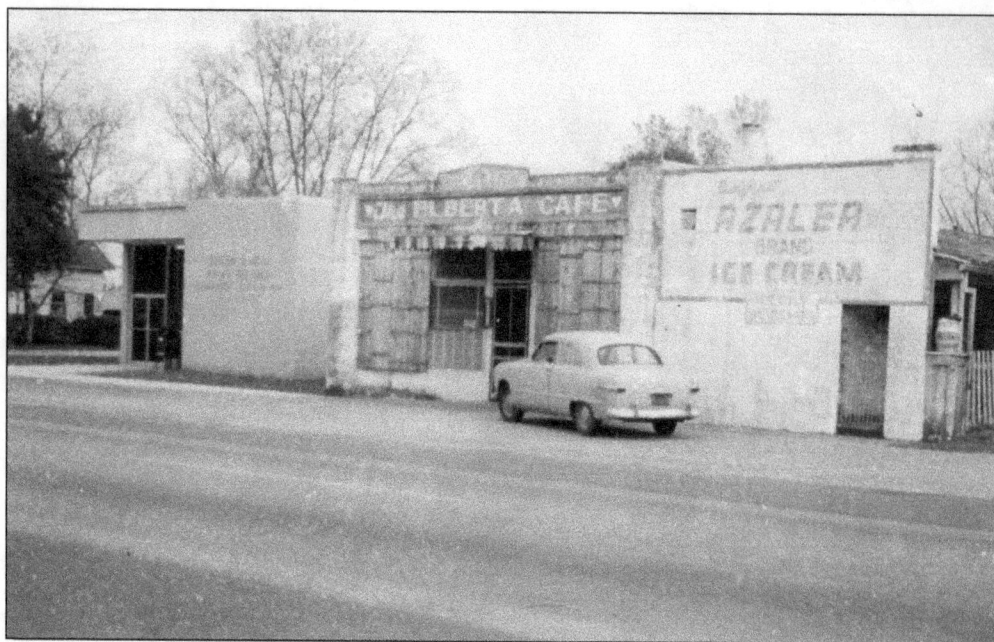

ELBERTA CAFÉ. The brick building pictured above was erected about 1920 by Martin Ehl, who ran a feed store there. Ten years later, Frank Mullek purchased it and also sold animal feed and farming supplies. When John Rhug bought the business, he opened a restaurant, but most residents remember the restaurant when it was later run by the Schweizers. The Elberta Café was so popular that parking was at a premium in town, especially on Saturdays. (Both, courtesy of Baldwin County Heritage Museum.)

ELBERTA FEED STORE. Erwin A. Koehler is pictured at the gas pump here at Elberta Feed Store. The store was opened as Elberta Feed Store in 1938. He started with Wayne Feeds, and then Pure Oil Company installed a gas pump, oil drum, and air compressor. Later, groceries and a few medical products were added to the store inventory. (Courtesy of Baldwin County Heritage Museum.)

KARL'S GENERAL STORE. The building first occupied by "Ma and Pa" Collier, on the corner of Main and State Streets, later became Bennie's Place and was known for its barbeque. Later, Edna and Karl Noltensmeier, pictured at left, ran a restaurant and general store in the building. Al Mullek redesigned the building by adding the two distinct towers that are there today. (Courtesy of Baldwin County Heritage Museum.)

ELBERTA MEAT LOCKER. A group of locals in 1945 saw a need for a business to prepare and freeze meat, and so they opened the Elberta Locker Plant. They processed all types of meat, and lockers in the freezer were rented to store meats and poultry. Alfred Stucki was manager of the plant from 1953 until his death in 1973. The plant closed its doors soon after. Pictured below in the 1960s are, from left to right, Clara Hertel, Alfred Stucki, Sanger Merchant, and Raymond Perry. The advertising slogan was "The People Pleasing Meat Company," and its heritage lives on in the recipe for the famous Elberta German sausages. (Both, courtesy of Baldwin County Heritage Museum.)

ST. MARK'S LUTHERAN. One of the earliest churches to be built in Elberta was organized in 1908, and the dedication of the little white church was in April 1909. The Lutheran services were held there until 1927, when the brick church was built. The wooden structure was still used as a Sunday school, parish hall, and storage until it was moved to the Baldwin County Heritage Museum in 1989. The first pastor was H.O. Bruss, and the first chairman was William Schreck. (Courtesy of Baldwin County Heritage Museum.)

TRINITY LUTHERAN. In 1907, the lovely white frame church pictured here was built on the corner of Main and Illinois Streets with the entrance on the south side. Trinity was a member of the Houston Conference, Texas District, of the American Lutheran Church, but few records remained after the church was destroyed by a tornado on March 31, 1933. The last minister was Rudolph Kohlrusch, who led services in homes of members after the tornado until he went into a Lutheran retirement home in 1935. (Courtesy of Baldwin County Heritage Museum.)

ROMAN CATHOLIC CHURCH. St. Bartholomew Catholic Church was built in 1910 on a parcel of five acres donated to the Mobile Diocese for the church and rectory by the Baldwin County Colonization Company in 1905. In order to best serve the local residents, a German-speaking priest from the St. Bernard Abbey in Cullman, Alabama, Fr. Gammelbert Brunner, was assigned to the parish. (Courtesy of Baldwin County Heritage Museum.)

ST. BENEDICT'S SCHOOL. A parochial school was built in Elberta in 1921 and staffed by Benedictine Sisters from Sacred Heart Convent in Cullman, Alabama. Students living far away were boarded at the school, and there was a stable to provide for mules and horses used by students who commuted. The sisters lived upstairs in the two-story building, and the students helped with chores needed to operate the school. (Courtesy of June Taylor.)

ELBERTA BAPTIST. In 1929, a group of 19 citizens organized the Baptist church and called Rev. J.A. Palmer as their first minister. The church met in homes of members until the building was constructed on land donated by Robert Bruhn on the corner of South Main and Olive Streets. After a new sanctuary was built in 1979, the original church was renovated to house the fellowship hall and educational classrooms (Courtesy of Baldwin County Heritage Museum.)

GOSPEL TABERNACLE CHURCH. The First Missionary Alliance Church was housed in a building constructed originally as temporary quarters for new settlers while building their farm homes. In 1923, the old wooden schoolhouse was purchased by the church and was named the Gospel Tabernacle. In 1927, they incorporated as Missionary Alliance. (Courtesy of Baldwin County Heritage Museum.)

FIRST SCHOOL. The children pictured here were among the earliest classes at the first school built in town on land donated and cleared by the Baldwin County Colonization Company. It was in the town center at the corner of Highways 98 and 83. Teachers were Louise Clark and Margaret Keueger. This school was sold to the Alliance Church and was moved to the back of the lot. (Courtesy of Baldwin County Heritage Museum.)

THREE-ROOM SCHOOLHOUSE. In 1919–1920, the seven small schools in the Elberta area were consolidated, and a new three-room school was built a few blocks north of the old building. Longtime principal N.P. Christensen organized the first PTA and oversaw the addition of classrooms for a junior high. The school was known for the beautiful rose garden, which was maintained by the principal and students. (Courtesy of Baldwin County Heritage Museum.)

1922 School Bus. With the consolidation of the seven area schools, many children needed transportation. Fred Ohls became the bus driver of a converted truck that had wooden seats and canvas shades for window coverings. At that time, bus drivers were contracted by the school system and provided their own vehicles. (Courtesy of Baldwin County Heritage Museum.)

Basketball Team. Basketball was the sport of choice for most girls. This photograph of the 1925 girls' team pictures, from left to right, (first row) Frieda Stucki, Regina Kaiser, Bonnie Keltz, and Bertha Koch; (second row) Elizabeth Neumann, Vena Brauhn, and Esther Stucki. (Courtesy of Baldwin County Heritage Museum.)

ELBERTA THIRD-GRADE CLASS. The 1945 class of Mildred Kleinschmidt poses in front of the 1920 building. Pictured from left to right are (first row) Shirley Jo Kinney, Joyce Doege, Audrey Neumann, Louise Resmondo, Glo Hadley, Shirley Ann McDuffie, Elinor Kaechele, Norma Riemer, Gerda Feil, and Carrie Good; (second row) Glenn Staimpel, William Smith, Earl Williams, Lillian Seitz, Gayle Brannon, Eva Leiterman, Bruce Willis, Leslie Pardue, and Henry Schult; (third row) Johnny Schaff, Richard Parker, Freddy Siebert, Mrs. Kleinschmidt, Richard Resmondo, Rudy Steiner, Jerry Klein, and Horace Watson. (Courtesy of Baldwin County Heritage Museum.)

FIFTH-GRADE PLAY. Teacher Rita Moore directed the play her fifth-grade students performed in 1948 at Elberta Consolidated School. Pictured from left to right are Audrey Neumann, Lillian Seitz, Elinor Kaechle, Henry Schult, Glo Hadley, Eva Leitermann, Myron Weaver, Carrie Good, Betty Ludeking, Shirley Jo Kinney, Gerda Feil, Joyce Doege, Norma Riemer, Shirley Ann McDuffie, Richard Parker, Bruce Willis, and Rudy Steiner. (Courtesy of Baldwin County Heritage Museum.)

MIFLIN BRIDGE. Just south of Elberta, the community of Miflin is the nearest point to the waters of Perdido Bay and on to the Gulf of Mexico. It was a boat landing for passengers, a supply depot for the area, and a popular swimming resort. The bridge was built over Miflin Creek to replace the ferry. (Courtesy of June Taylor.)

SWIFT PRESBYTERIAN CHURCH. South of Elberta, near Miflin, Charles and Ira Swift ran a lumber mill on Sandy Creek. The brothers married sisters of the Roberts family in Mobile, and many Roberts family members moved to Baldwin County. Miriam Swift envisioned a Presbyterian church, and with land donated by the Swift family, a church was built in 1907, originally named the Little Church in the Piney Woods. (Courtesy of Foley Museum.)

OLD MIFLIN SCHOOL. The one-room school at Miflin, pictured above, served local students as well as those who would come by boat. It was replaced about 1920 with the three-room building in the background of the photograph below. The girls pictured are members of the 4H Club, the most popular of all school organizations. The older building was moved to the Baldwin County Heritage Museum as a school museum, and the school seen below remains in use as a community center for the town of Miflin. (Above, courtesy of Baldwin County Historical Development Commission; below, courtesy of Baldwin County Heritage Museum.)

PERDIDO BEACH SCHOOL. Perdido Beach was one of the earliest settlements in Baldwin County, with its good harbor on Perdido Bay. The one-room school photograph was taken in 1909. From left to right are (first row) Inez Kinmon, Ruth Resmondo, Claud Kinmon, Nellie White, Rufus Kee, Willie Kinmon, Sidney Resmondo, ? Best, Jimmie Parker, and Fletcher Key; (second row) Ed Kerr, William Resmondo, Carrie Parker, Dolph Suarez, Guy While, Tommy Best, George Kinmon, Alvis Key, and Augustine Resmondo; (third row) teacher Edna Peadro, Elma Suarez, Emery Best, Lyria Davis, John Climie,Tommy Davis, Edna Best, Jesse Resmondo, Nettie Parker, and Dergis Resmondo. (Courtesy of Baldwin County Heritage Museum.)

PIRATES COVE. Nearby in the community of Josephine, the property around Robert's Bayou, also known as Pirates' Cove, was developed by Max Lawrenz, who came to Baldwin County in 1916. The store pictured above was managed by Fred and Elsa Noltensmeier in the 1940s, and the porches around the store afforded places to watch bathers and boats along the intracoastal waterway. (Courtesy of Baldwin County Heritage Museum.)

STATE BANK OF ELBERTA

ELBERTA
04   195

SOUTH BALDWIN
CHAMBER · COMMERCE

SOUTHLAND SKETCHES   by Walter Overton

ELBERTA

PRAYING
MANTIS SHRIMP
18 INCHES LONG
THE USUAL LENGTH OF THIS
SPECIES IS 2 TO 4 INCHES.
— Owned by
JAMES T. PETERSON
Panama City
Florida

SKETCHED HERE FROM AN OLD PHOTOGRAPH
IS A SCENE AT THE INTERSECTION OF THE TWO
CENTRAL MAIN STREETS OF THE MODERN, IN-
CORPORATED TOWN OF ELBERTA, ALA.,
AS IT WAS IN 1904. TODAY, A TRAFFIC
LIGHT IS SUSPENDED WHERE THE
SIGN IS SHOWN AND BUSY TRAFFIC
MOVES IN FOUR DIRECTIONS
UNDER IT.

CODEN, ALABAMA
WAS SO NAMED BY THE
FRENCH ON ACCOUNT OF
THE GREAT NUMBER OF
WILD TURKEYS
FOUND THERE IN
EARLY DAYS

THE NAME WAS, ORIGINALLY,
COQ D'INDE (TURKEY), BUT
OVER THE YEARS, AS THEY PASSED,
IT FINALLY TURNED INTO CODEN.

GOLDEN JUBILEE 1954. The town of Elberta faithfully celebrates, with great fervor, its town history every 25 years. The 50th-anniversary event featured the parade shown in this photograph. The Bank of Elberta, in the back of the picture, was started by the earliest settlers and was one of the few banks in the county that did not have to close its doors during the Depression years. (Courtesy of Baldwin County Heritage Museum.)

FIRST TOWN SIGN. Walter Overton paid tribute to Elberta in his weekly "Southland Sketches" in local newspapers. He shows the town sign from the earliest days in 1904. (Courtesy of Baldwin County Department of Archives and History.)

72

Five

BON SECOUR

SWIFT CONSOLIDATED SCHOOL. This 1920 school was built on five acres acquired from the Charles Swift family and consolidated several area schools. Students in grades one through eight attended the three-room school. The campus included a teacherage and a home occupied by the principal and his or her family. The bell in the school was rung manually and remains at the school, which still operates today. (Courtesy of June Taylor.)

FRIENDSHIP BAPTIST CHURCH. Started with Sunday school in the home of Lou Cooper, the group decided to build a Baptist church and hired D.C. Arthur, who donated the land for the church near the river. To finance the 1925 church, members each planted an acre crop for the church, and they had raised money to pay for the building by 1929. (Photograph by Penny H. Taylor.)

OLD EPISCOPAL CHURCH. St. Peter's by the Bay was called "God's Lighthouse" by mariners because they followed the steeple cross by day and a lantern on the flagpole by night to find their way into the Bon Secour River. The 1885 church was at the entrance to the "safe harbor," which is the meaning of Bon Secour. It withstood hurricanes in 1906, 1916, and 1926, but a fire claimed it in 1928. (Courtesy of Swift-Coles Historic Home.)

OUR LADY OF BON SECOUR CATHOLIC CHURCH. The family of Jacques Cook had firmly established the Catholic community by 1830 and donated land for the Cook cemetery across the road from his homestead in 1835. The church was first built across the river in 1890, but after 1916 storm damage, it was dismantled and moved to the spot on which the Nicholas Cook house had stood, donated by Odile Cook Bertrand. (Courtesy of Foley Museum.)

METHODIST CHURCH. The earliest building of the Methodist church was this wooden structure; however, it was later abandoned. Later on, it also was a Nazarene church for a few years. When Clay Grant came to Bon Secour and found the abandoned building and cemetery, he initiated the project to restore it and reclaim the cemetery. Today, it is Morgan's Chapel United Methodist Church. (Courtesy of Baldwin County Historical Development Commission.)

COMMISSARY STORE. A store was built by Charles Swift to serve as the commissary store for the workers in his lumber mill on the property. It was managed by Benjamin F. Patterson, who is pictured with his son Norvell on the front porch, which faces the riverbank. These photographs were taken during World War I, and posters calling for enlistment in the Navy are displayed. Below, inside the store, young Norvell poses near the military banner indicating that a member of the family is serving in the war. (Both, courtesy of Swift-Coles Historic Home.)

SWIFT STORE. After the lumber mill closed, a store operated for a while by members of the Swift family served the community. Most deliveries were still made by boat until the 1940s, when the roads were improved. In the early days, the mail from Elberta had to go to Mobile by train and then by boat to Bon Secour, taking at least two weeks. (Courtesy of Swift-Coles Historic Home.)

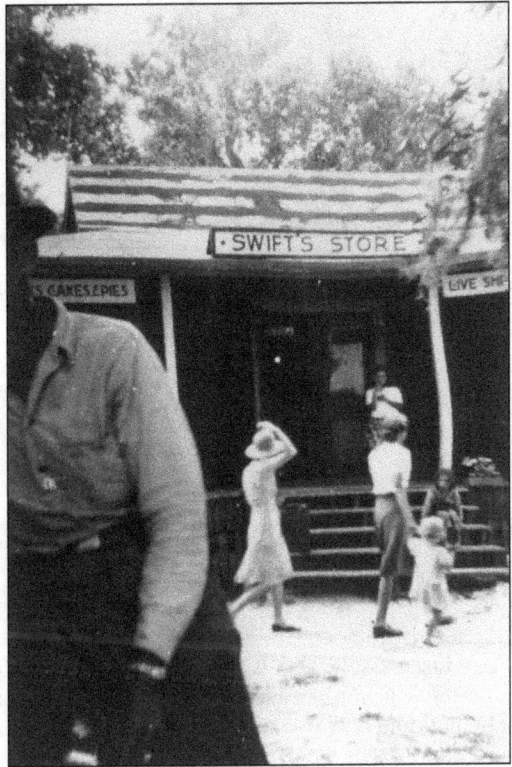

INSIDE STORE. When the commissary store was once again run by the Patterson family, brother and sister Norvell and Dorothy were always on hand to serve customers. Here, neighbor Ione Swift Jurkiewicz is shown carrying her daughter Mary Robin inside the store about 1962. Also pictured are Norvell Patterson and Dorothy Patterson. (Courtesy of Swift-Coles Historic Home.)

POST OFFICE. The flag is flying over the building that served as the post office for many years. Charles Wakeford and his wife, "Meme" (Amelia), who lived in the house as well, operated it. The building had also housed a store at one time. Meme Wakeford was the daughter of Charles and Susan Swift. (Courtesy of June Taylor.)

MEME'S RESTAURANT. Charles and Meme Wakeford lived in the large family home on the river during World War II and were known to open their home to servicemen stationed nearby for fresh seafood dinners. After the war, they opened a restaurant named simply Meme's. It became famous throughout the nation. (Courtesy of Swift-Coles Historic Home.)

ST. PETER'S. In 1932, just a few years after the wooden church had burned, the Episcopal church pictured was built on land donated by Susan Roberts Swift next to the Swift Consolidated School. A parish hall was added in 1950, and a cemetery is located immediately behind the church. (Photograph by Penny H. Taylor.)

VACATION BIBLE SCHOOL. Children of Bon Secour pose for a photograph during vacation Bible school at St. Peter's Episcopal Church. At least one year, the summer event was held at the Swift home, where Susan Swift served refreshments to the children. Picture from left to right are (first row) Sidney Howard, Clinton Anderson, and Arvie Allen; (second row) two unidentified children, Shannon Blackwell, and Debbie Miller. (Courtesy of Swift-Coles Historic Home.)

OYSTER HOUSE. The earliest seafood businesses in Bon Secour focused on harvesting oysters. Oysters were gathered from private beds and public reefs, kept alive in pens offshore, and brought to large oyster houses, as seen above, for loading on vessels bound for Mobile. Production averaged 650 barrels per week during the oyster season, which includes all months with an *R* in the name. (Courtesy of Swift-Coles Historic Home.)

OYSTER SHELLS. With refrigeration improvement, oysters were shucked on site and packaged for transport. Products, which now included fish and shrimp, were shipped by boat to Mobile or by rail from the Foley station. The resulting oyster shell mounds were common sights all along the banks of the river. Area homes often used the shells for covering driveways. (Courtesy of Swift-Coles Historic Home.)

BON SECOUR FISHERIES. Frank Nelson came from Denmark in 1896 and founded a business at Oyster Bay that is today's Bon Secour Fisheries, Inc. Operated by three generations of the Nelson family, the operation moved to the location here in 1939. An ice plant was built, and the business grew to include shrimp boats, a packaging plant, and delivery trucks. (Courtesy of Baldwin County Heritage Museum.)

WEEKS GAZEBO. George Brown's home and gardens on Bon Secour River were well known locally for the beautiful gazebo, or "shoe-fly," he built around an ancient oak tree. The structure was the setting for many weddings held in the gardens, where the Spanish moss hangs from the trees. The gazebo was badly damaged in Hurricane Frederic in 1979 but was restored and hosted a wedding there two weeks after the storm. However, Hurricane Ivan in 2005 completely destroyed the landmark. (Courtesy of Baldwin County Heritage Museum.)

WEEKS COTTAGE. Thought to be the home of Nicholas Weekes on Weeks Bay, the cottage was moved to Bon Secour in 1970 by George Brown. The first Catholic mass locally was held in the home of the French Weekes family. George Brown restored the cabin and furnished it with period antiques. The Browns' main home and gazebo have been damaged by hurricanes, but the cottage remains intact. (Courtesy of Baldwin County Heritage Museum.)

TABBY FOUNDATION. The earliest homes were built of tabby, a material made of oyster shells, sand, ash, water, and limestone. The remains of a tabby building, pictured above, were found in the Bon Secour area and are known as the "mystery fort." (Courtesy of Baldwin County Historic Development Commission.)

THE MARYETTA. Frank Nelson acquired the 50-foot converted schooner named the *MaryEtta* in 1896 for use as an oyster dredger, transporter, and shrimp boat. The vessel's keel was laid in 1860, and it was launched as the *Curlew*, which had only one mast. A second mast was added at a later date to make it equal to its competitor oyster-harvesting vessels. (Courtesy of Baldwin County Heritage Museum.)

AFTER HURRICANE FREDERIC. When John A. Nelson joined his father in the business in 1920, a 16-horsepower engine was added to the boat. The boat was retired in 1969 and was docked on the banks of the Bon Secour River. Ten years later, the devastating Hurricane Frederic damaged it past repair. (Courtesy of Baldwin County Historical Development Commission.)

SOUTHLAND SKETCHES   by Walter Overton

So
Be
SOY
BEANS
OY
EANS
OY
ANS

THE FIRST SOY BEANS
GROWN IN SOUTH ALABAMA
ARE SAID TO HAVE BEEN SOLD TO
THE FORD MOTOR CO. TO BE USED
IN MAKING STEERING-WHEELS,
DOOR HANDLES, ETC.
SOY BEANS ARE
NOW A MAJOR
SOUTH ALABAMA CROP.

BON SECOUR
SEAFOODS
Bonito
- ENJOYED IN THE MOBILE BAY AREA
FOR MORE THAN 250 YEARS—HAVE IN
RECENT YEARS BECOME NATIONALLY
FAMOUS, AND "BON SECOUR" SEAFOODS ARE
NOW SERVED IN CHICAGO AND NEW YORK,
AND ARE CALLED FOR BY NAME IN THE BETTER
RESTAURANTS.
MULLET

SIGSBEE'S DEEP
—A TREMENDOUS "SINK" IN
THE FLOOR OF THE GULF OF
MEXICO — IS 100 MILES WIDE
AND 300 MILES LONG, WITH AN
ALMOST UNIFORM DEPTH OF
12,000 FEET.
THE WALLS ARE OF APPALLING DEPTH
AND SHEERNESS, DROPPING STRAIGHT
DOWN FROM THE GULF-BOTTOM LEVEL.

WALTER OVERTON. A popular feature in publications along the Gulf Coast was the work of author and artist Walter Overton, who lived in Bon Secour for more than 30 years. He authored several books, was a respected watercolorist, and wrote and illustrated the "Southland Sketches." He created the feature from interesting tidbits he picked up locally and from articles mailed to him. He is pictured above working at his desk about 1976, shortly before his death. The at left below shows one of the cartoons in which he mentioned the growth of the seafood industry in his hometown. (Both, courtesy of Baldwin County Department of Archives and History.)

Six

HOME ON THE RIVER

ORIGINAL SWIFT SCHOOL. The Charles and Susan Swift family had moved to the beautiful home on the Bon Secour River by 1900. They soon built this one-room school for their children and the children of the mill workers. Posing with some of the students is teacher Emily Swift, a daughter of Charles and Susan. (Courtesy of Swift-Coles Historic Home.)

MAM-MAW'S EASTER LILIES. When the Charles and Susan Swift family moved to Bon Secour, they purchased a home from Thomas Gavin and moved there with eight children. The home was a one-story dogtrot-style cabin, but the Swifts added a large two-room wing to the west side of the house. Susan Swift was known for her lovely Easter lilies and hospitality. (Courtesy of Swift-Coles Historic Home.)

SWEPT GARDEN PATHS. Surrounding the home was a picket fence to keep the free-range cattle and other livestock out of the immediate house gardens. A maze of paths was designed around the gardens, bordered by lovely flowering plants and shrubs. (Courtesy of Swift-Coles Historic Home.)

BARNYARD AND CHICKEN COOP. To the rear of the house was the barn and chicken coop, where the Swift children shared in the chores of milking the cow and gathering the eggs. Like most Bon Secour residents, the Swift family was almost self-sufficient in the days of difficult travel. (Courtesy of Swift-Coles Historic Home.)

FIVE-SEATER OUTHOUSE. Before indoor plumbing, the outhouse was necessary—in this case, a rare one with five seats! One of the seats was in a separate compartment; therefore, a little privacy was available. Other outbuildings included a smokehouse, corncrib, the first kitchen, and a house for a housekeeper. (Courtesy of Swift-Coles Historic Home.)

SWIFT TIDEWATER HOME. As the family grew to a total of 11 children, Charles Swift decided to add a second story to the house, which was completed by 1910. A family diary records that a builder was engaged to assure that the foundation could support the addition. The house was increased to 16 rooms in 6,000 square feet, with more than 3,000 square feet in covered porches. The photograph above shows the south side of the house, and one below shows the southeast corner view. (Both, courtesy of Swift-Coles Historic Home.)

MILL AT BON SECOUR

SWIFT LUMBER MILL. At the intersection of Schoolhouse Creek and Bon Secour River, Charles Swift built a lumber mill to process the thousands of longleaf pine trees growing on the land he had purchased on either side of the river. The Swifts also had mills at Nolte Creek, Perdido Bay, Miflin, Seminole, and in Ellisville and Chicoura, Mississippi. (Courtesy of Swift-Coles Historic Home.)

NARROW-GAUGE RAIL. The Swift brothers also had a mill at nearby Miflin. A railroad was used to transport logs to both mills, and extensive railroad lines were constructed, as seen in this trestle structure. Pictured from left to right are Robin Swift, John Lewis, and an unidentified engineer in 1912. (Courtesy of Swift-Coles Historic Home.)

SWIFT SCHOOLHOUSE. The first wooden schoolhouse was built soon after the Swifts moved to Bon Secour, and daughter Emily taught there. Pictured are the boys preparing for a baseball game. After a new three-room school was built in 1920, the old building was used for various purposes and eventually was the home of the Norell family. (Courtesy of Swift-Coles Historic Home.)

BALDWIN RIVERBOAT. Riverboats and bay boats were common sights in the early days of Bon Secour. Here is pictured the *Baldwin*, a passenger boat that ran from Mobile to Pensacola with several bay and river stops, including the old Henrietta Hotel at Palmetto Beach and Swift's landing in Bon Secour. One of its early skippers was Capt. Buck Curran. (Courtesy of Swift-Coles Historic Home.)

FISH FRY ON THE RIVER. The caption inscribed on the photograph above says, "War Time Picnic and Fish Fry Bon Secour, Alabama. Given by S.D. Gaar Campaign Committee. July 17, 1918. Fresh, crisp fish and plenty of them." The window is painted with a plea to buy a Tom and Kitty and help the Red Cross. (Courtesy of Swift-Coles Historic Home.)

PICNIC FUN AND FOOD. The wharf located at the river landing of the Swift home was the location of many social gatherings. Here, under the shade of the famous live oak trees bedecked in Spanish moss, townsfolk gather to share in a potluck picnic. (Courtesy of Swift-Coles Historic Home.)

SWIFT FAMILY CHILDREN. Charles and Susan Swift reared 11 children in their lovely home in Bon Secour. Here, all 11 siblings are gathered for a photograph in 1910. From left to right are (first row) Susan Nell, Ira, Polly, Meme, Edward, and Bydie; (second row) Emily, Robin, Eleanor, William Henry, and Miriam. (Courtesy of Swift-Coles Historic Home.)

THREE ELDEST GIRLS. The three Swift sisters in this formal portrait are, from left to right, Miriam, Emily, and Eleanor. Miriam married Lyman Martyn, taught school, and eventually moved to Miami. Emily taught school in the Swift School for several years, moved to Mobile for a while, but returned to the family home in 1939 to care for her niece Ione. Eleanor taught music and married Roger Stevens, raising two children in Mobile. (Courtesy of Ione Swift Jurkiewicz.)

SUSAN CORNELIA SWIFT. Susan Swift is pictured here at age 16 while on a visit to an aunt in Mobile. Susan married Randy Marshall, lived in Mobile, but returned to the family home in 1949. She lived in the home until her death in 1976 and was the last Swift family member to live in the home. (Courtesy of Swift-Coles Historic Home.)

FAMILY PORTRAIT IN THE PARLOR. In the front parlor, members of the Swift family pose for a photograph about 1909. Pictured from left to right are (first row) Susan Platt Roberts Swift, Amelia "Meme" Swift, John Byard Swift, and Charles Augustus Swift; (second row) Louise DuBose Roberts Swift, Ira Austin Swift Sr., Eleanor Bowie Swift, Miriam Roberts Swift, and Ira Platt Swift. (Courtesy of Ione Swift Jurkiewicz.)

DONKEY RIDE. Children created their entertainment in the early days. Here are pictured Ira and Byard Swift riding the donkeys. In adulthood, Ira became a brigadier general in World War II. Byard moved to Atmore, where he operated a farm and was involved in the mill business with his brother Robin. Robin also served as a state and US senator. (Courtesy of Swift-Coles Historic Home.)

LOVEBIRDS. The unidentified couple striking a charming pose on the donkey cart typifies the weekend gatherings that took place often at the river home. Friends from school and from Mobile often came to spend time with the Swift family. Susan Swift was known for her hospitality. However, young men were housed exclusively in the rooms upstairs on the left, called the "Boar's Den." (Courtesy of Swift-Coles Historic Home.)

RIVER COTTAGE. The Swift family had several cottages along the river that were rented out as fishing cabins. Edward operated the cottage business and a store for several years. Eventually, four of the five cottages were moved across the river to Swift's landing. (Courtesy of Swift-Coles Historic Home.)

LITTLE IONE. The only grandchild to have lived in the home was Ione, born to William Henry and Ione Swift. Her aunt Emily moved back from Mobile to help care for her while Ione's mother served as principal of Swift School. After World War II, the family moved to the teacherage on the school campus. (Courtesy of Ione Swift Jurkiewicz.)

Building County Road 10. Until the 1920s, river transportation was the most viable option. When the county began paving roads, such as shown in the photograph, automobiles were able to make the journey to the river homes more readily. Electricity, however, did not reach Bon Secour until 1937. (Courtesy of Swift-Coles Historic Home.)

Sept 1926

The Insect, 1926. William H. "Billy" Swift, Edward "Kiddo" Swift, and cousin John B. Swift are pictured from left to right upon their arrival in Miami, Florida. The car, nicknamed "the Insect," was built entirely by Johnnie, and the three drove the car from the Swift home in Bon Secour to Miami to visit Miriam Swift Martyn and family, a trip of 712 miles. The young boy in the back of the photograph is Lyman Martyn. (Courtesy of Sandra Swift Straughn, daughter of John Swift.)

NIK COLES. In 1976, the Swift home was sold to Nik Coles, a local businessman who ran the Friendship House Restaurant in Gulf Shores. He lived in the home until his death in 2007, at which time the home was bequeathed to the Baldwin County Historical Development Commission, which operates the home as a museum. (Courtesy of Swift-Coles Historic Home.)

HISTORY PRESERVED. The iron horse hitching posts line the drive of the magnificent home on the Bon Secour River, which opens its arms to welcome guests just as it has done for more than 100 years. The historic grounds give a respite from the busy world in an idyllic setting, validating the lovely name "Safe Harbor." (Courtesy of Swift-Coles Historic Home.)

97

FISHING IN MOBILE BAY AT THE MOUTH OF BON SECOUR RIVER, W^M A. SWIFT, OF BON SECOUR HOOKED AND "BOATED" A TARPON THAT WON A PRIZE IN A NATIONAL FIELD AND STREAM CONTEST IN WHICH ONLY SIX PRIZES WERE AWARDED. (LENGTH 7FT, 2 INCHES. WEIGHT, 138 LBS.)

SIXTY-FOUR DOLLARS FOR ONE MOBILE BAY FISH... NOT BAD!

A STURGEON TAKEN AT MULLET POINT YIELDED 60 POUNDS OF CAVIAR AND BROUGHT

BON SECOUR SKETCHES. One of the "Southland Sketches" by Walter Overton mentioned the *Baldwin*, a riverboat that made regular landings at Mobile, Fairhope, Zundels, Magnolia Springs, Swift, Miflin, and Pensacola. The foredeck reference in the article below made it unusual. Actually, the upper deck was modified in later years to try to compensate for the top-heavy build. The photograph above includes an article about the prize-winning tarpon caught by William "Billy" Swift of Bon Secour. (Both, courtesy of Baldwin County Department of Archives and History.)

by Walter Overton

ANOTHER FRIEND FROM OTHER DAYS —THE BALDWIN, BORE A FAMILIAR NAME.

The "BALDWIN"

THE WATERS OF THE BAY KNEW HER WELL, AND AT ONE TIME SHE MADE STOPS ON FISH RIVER AS FAR UP AS THE STORE AT GROVE'S LANDING AT MARLOW. HER FORE-DECK EXTENDED SO FAR AHEAD OF HER HOUSING THAT IN A STRONG SIDE WIND SWEEPS WERE USED TO HELP IN KEEPING HER ON HER COURSE.

Seven

MAGNOLIA SPRINGS

YUPON UNDERWOOD SCHOOL, 1914–1916. Schools have been important to Magnolia Springs since 1876, when schools for both Creole and white children began. The early 1900s saw two schools open; they were consolidated in 1932 into one that operated for 30-plus years. In 1937, the Richard Kelly Frank School came to be on land donated by Maurice Frank. (Courtesy of Foley Library.)

THE EARLY SPRINGS AND A WISHING WELL. The Baldwin County Commission has designated the springs as part of the county's park system, making it the third historic park and 18th park in Baldwin County. Many natural springs flow year-round with water quality of the purest to be found in nature. Several chemical testing companies from Chicago certified the pureness around 1900. To add to the allure and attractiveness of the park, a wooden cage-like wishing well enclosure was built surrounding the well whereby visitors wished for a particular outcome and usually made a monetary donation, paying a price to the well-dweller or well-guardian to ensure their wish would come true. (Above, courtesy of the Foley Museum; below, courtesy of Magnolia Springs City Hall.)

FIRST HOME IN THE SPRINGS, 1871. With land selling for about 50¢ per acre, Lizzie Breed and her son opened an inn that still stands today. It is called a plantation house with its wraparound porch, or gallery, for protection from both hot sun and heavy rain. Nearby was the overseer's cottage and quarters for house servants. (Courtesy of Baldwin County Heritage Museum.)

WATERMELONS TO NEW ORLEANS BY WATER, 1927. From this early beginning, farm produce was shipped by boat to New Orleans into the 1950s until it became cheaper to ship by truck. Each boat handled four to five truckloads of watermelons, minus the ones the local boys, hired as loaders, dropped and ate. (Courtesy of Weeks Bay National Estuarine Research Reserve.)

HUEY COLLINS, WATER ROUTE CARRIER.
"Neither snow nor rain nor heat nor
gloom of night"—this is the unofficial
creed of the post office. The words would
be different in Magnolia Springs—
"Neither waves nor tides nor hurricane
rains"—because the mail still comes by
boat. (Courtesy of Jeannie Collins.)

FIRST US POST OFFICE, 1878. The Magnolia Plantation received its mail from Fairhope by horse
and buggy until 1916, when residents along the Magnolia River, Weeks Bay, and Fish River had
mail delivered by boat. Now known as the Magnolia Springs Post Office, mail is still delivered
via a water route. (Courtesy of Magnolia Springs City Hall.)

COMMUNITY CENTER. Once a month, after a potluck meal on the first Saturday, the association holds a meeting, following in the footsteps of the tradition started in 1927; "no meeting months" are June, July, August, and September. The association's strategic plan is simple, having two objectives: fellowship and activity. (Courtesy of Penny H. Taylor.)

F.N. ALLEN'S 1894 TOWN HALL. Hats are off in tribute to the following early residents who contributed to town hall's construction: Otis Lyman, Fred Babcock, F.N. Allens, William Howes, Frank Brunnels, Horace Dunbars, Daisy Thompson, Will Dowty, Gertrude Smith, and her mother, Ida Gates. (Courtesy of Penny H. Taylor.)

ST. JOHN'S CATHOLIC CHURCH, 1902. Little did the parishioners and builders of the church know that in a few years the major 1906 hurricane would strike the church to the ground. Not to be intimidated by the weather, the church was rebuilt, only to suffer complete devastation in the monster hurricane of 1916; it was rebuilt again with renovations in the late 1940s. (Courtesy of Jeannie Collins.)

CONSECRATION OF ST. PAUL'S EPISCOPAL CHAPEL, 1902. Keeping with its original design—heart pine frame construction, 27 feet by 51 feet, with a plain wooden cross and altar and a seating capacity of 80—St. Paul's underwent needed repairs in 1963 along with additions to create its current profile. (Courtesy of Penny H. Taylor.)

THE 1942 WESLEYAN CHURCH.
With world headquarters
in Indiana, the church was
founded in 1968, formed from
mergers of like-minded groups
dating back to 1843 and John
Wesley's Methodism. Traditional
service and a modern worship
service serve its communicants
each Sunday. It now has a
second sanctuary addition.
(Courtesy of Penny H. Taylor.)

VERNANT PARK BAPTIST CHURCH. The church was organized in 1928 by Albert Lipscomb, a Baptist from Demopolis who bought property in Weeks Bay and donated land for a church. Church services were held in the Magnolia Springs Community Hall until 1933, when the parishioners moved to a small building in Vernant Park. A larger building was built in 1937 that was later replaced by an even larger building. (Courtesy of Penny H. Taylor.)

ONE OF MAGNOLIA SPRINGS'S FIRST STORES, C. 1903. Frequent ownership changes marked the steady progression of location changes, floods, fires, and an "institution" called Moores' Store, which operated from 1922 to 1993. Early family names associated with general stores were the Schindlers, Nick Sawyer, George and Arthur Holk, and Gray and Mac Moore. (Courtesy of Weeks Bay National Estuarine Research Reserve.)

MOORE BROTHERS' STORE, 1951. From its origins in 1922, Gray Moore and impresario Jessie King worked there every day for 30 years and never missed a shift; the general store was the center for news, views, fixings for stews, and humble work boots. They had it all. (Courtesy of Foley Museum.)

STEAMSHIP MAGNOLIA. Jump aboard to take a day trip to Mobile or pick up one's inbound produce or fruit from the *Magnolia*. Steam-powered ships expanded river travel from the late 1800s until the 1927 Mobile-Baldwin County Causeway ended their reign and the automobile and truck became the transportation of choice. (Courtesy of Weeks Bay National Estuarine Research Reserve.)

STEAMSHIP NEW MAGNOLIA. The addition to the fleet was a much larger vessel with two decks, separating the freight on the lower deck with passengers on the upper. Tragically, in 1934, the *New Magnolia* was overcome by fire like its sister ship and perished at the dock in Grove's Landing at Marlow on Fish River. (Courtesy of Weeks Bay National Estuarine Research Reserve.)

E.Y. HORDER. E.Y. Horder built at least two structures in Magnolia Springs. Horder, a Chicagoan, made his first trip to Magnolia Springs in 1908; the trip took at least 30 hours by railroad, steamship, and finally, a mule-driven covered van. The wealthy Horder visited Magnolia Springs many times. The first house he built was a guesthouse used by many visitors over the years. The large compound, last owned by H.G. Horder, was in the style of the time and constructed for the Southern climate and featured a covered porch surrounding the interior rooms with wide hallways and large windows to let the air flow through on those dog days of summer before air-conditioning. No doubt arriving in March after several months of Chicago winters was most welcome. (Both, courtesy of Magnolia Springs City Hall.)

THE OAK PARKER PLEASURE BOAT, MAGNOLIA SPRINGS. Here is E.Y. Horder's fishing boat on the Magnolia River. The fishing pole and reel are ready for a big catch: an alligator gar tipping the scale at 70 pounds, a 110-pound tarpon, or record-sized red fish. What more could a guest from Chicago ask for in March? (Courtesy of Magnolia Springs City Hall.)

SUNNYSIDE HOTEL. Christopher McLennan, a Chicagoan, built the hotel in 1897 and used it as a hunting lodge. Several owners bought and sold it until William Harding opened the property for guests as the Sunnyside Hotel. The hotel outlived the Hardings. (Courtesy of Weeks Bay National Estuarine Research Reserve.)

THE WOODBOUND HOTEL, C. 1895. The following accommodations seem beyond belief to the present day: with 126 galleries, rooms faced an outdoor covered hall complete with rocking chairs; on the river side, rooms with a view had baths and running water, and each room was warmed with a gas heater and lighted by gas. Charges were from $1.50 to $2 a day, including room and board with use of the bath. In addition, cottages adjoining the hotel with four to six rooms and kitchens could be rented. Air-conditioning did not exist, so breezes and the hotel's design kept the patrons comfortable. (Both, courtesy of Weeks Bay National Estuarine Research Reserve.)

THE WOODBOUND HOTEL SALES BROCHURE. The fame of the hotel was short-lived due to a lightning strike from a thunderstorm, burning the main building to the ground in 1911. The L&N Railroad had many major departure cities from the Midwest "all aboard" for an easy trip with "Unexcelled Dining Car Service." (Courtesy of Weeks Bay National Estuarine Research Reserve.)

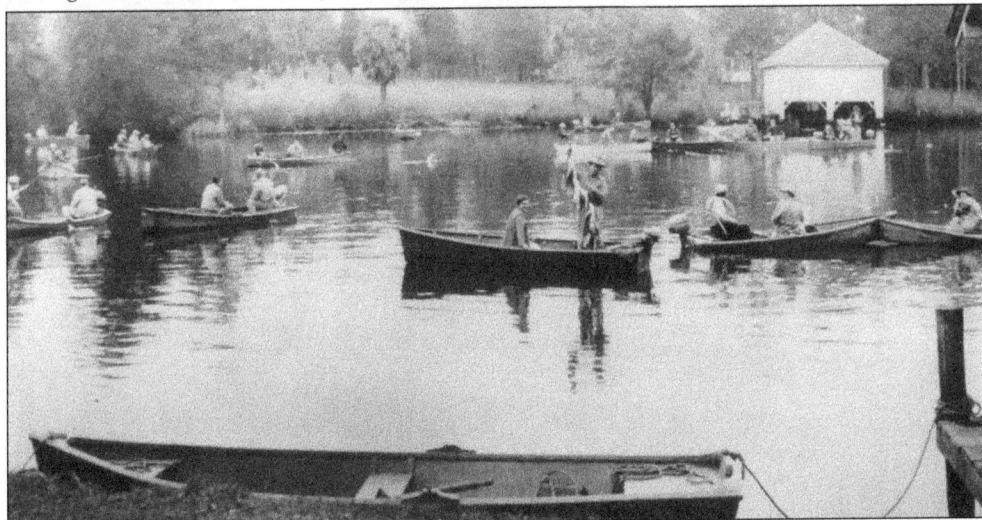

THE DEVIL'S HOLE, 1954. Found long ago, the hole's bottom was not to be plumbed. Years later, several measurements were made, successfully finding the bottom. Because of its depth, ice-cold waters, and location, fishermen found out that the devil did not live there, but lots of fish did. (Courtesy of Weeks Bay National Estuarine Research Reserve.)

SOUTH LODGE OF GOVERNOR'S CLUB, 1900s. Building started around 1905 for Frank Brunnel, a wealthy man from Chicago and New York, and continued for years, adding several cottages and a brick silo. In 1923, the State of Alabama purchased the main house, three clubhouses, and five cottages, which became known as the Governor's Club and were used as a hunting and fishing getaway. (Courtesy of Weeks Bay National Estuarine Research Reserve.)

GOVERNOR'S CLUB, EAST SIDE, MAGNOLIA RIVER. Narrow punt-like rowboats made fishing for the record setter easy by finding the right "hole" and quietly casting one's bait. Many varieties of fish made their way into the river from Mobile Bay through Weeks Bay. Standing up in the narrow boat was not recommended. (Courtesy of Weeks Bay National Estuarine Research Reserve.)

SACK RACE, FOURTH OF JULY. Following the annual Fourth of July parade were games for children and adults. With both feet in a sack, the first one to hop to the finish line was declared the winner. (Courtesy of Weeks Bay National Estuarine Research Reserve.)

THE FORT MORGAN AND MAGNOLIA SPRINGS ALL-STAR TEAMS. One of Gray Moore's contributions to Magnolia Springs was its baseball team. He paid expenses to recruit high-caliber players. Sunday afternoon baseball flourished before and after World War II on the local field. Television broadcasting of baseball caused the decline of county leagues. (Courtesy of Foley Museum.)

YUPON FARM BARN. Vestiges of German, English, and Swedish design are in the barn's construction. This form includes an overhung loft with ventilation soffits and the gambrel-style roof—the word "gambrel" being derived from the hock of a horse's leg. The roof slants sharply in two different pitches, allowing the rain to drain off quickly as well as providing greater room in the loft. (Courtesy of Baldwin County Department of Archives and History.)

YUPON, ALABAMA, JULY 5, 1923. The area is so named for a holly shrub (also spelled "yaupon") growing in the area whose leaves are brewed as a bitter tea. Trees—oaks and pines—were a mainstay of the economy, providing lumber and turpentine exports to many states via the Fish and Magnolia Rivers into Weeks Bay. (Courtesy of Magnolia Springs City Hall.)

114

WEEKS BAY PITCHER PLANT BOG. Bogs bring together a unique combination of water, soil, and environmental conditions not as wet as other wetland habitats, like swamps and marshes. The bog's ecosystem is dependent on recurring fires—usually lightning—to suppress the growth of shrubs and trees. Many of its indigenous plants are found nowhere else on earth. (Courtesy of Penny H. Taylor.)

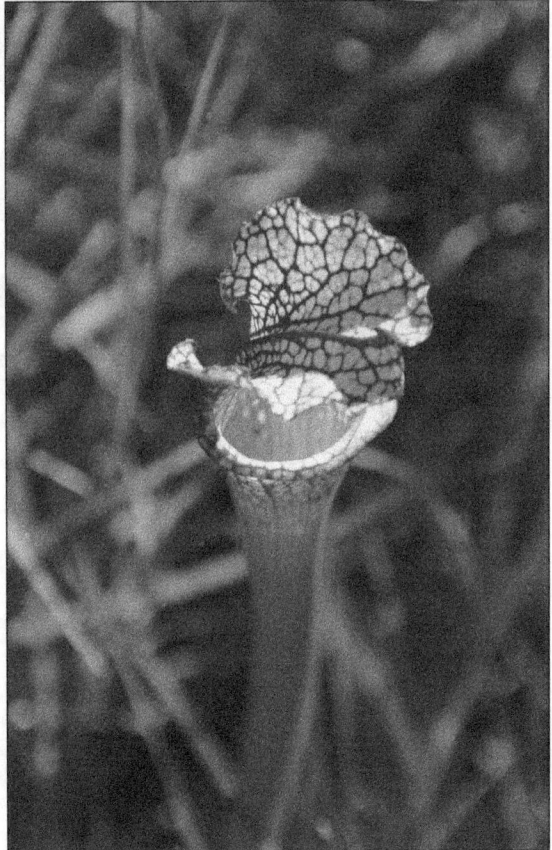

A PITCHER PLANT. The white-topped pitcher plant grows in a very restricted area from Appalachicola, Florida, along the coastal plain to Louisiana. The large bell mouth and leaves attract insects and other small creatures into the hollow tube, from which they cannot escape. A pool of digestive enzymes feed the plant minerals and nutrients from the decomposed insect. (Courtesy of Penny H. Taylor.)

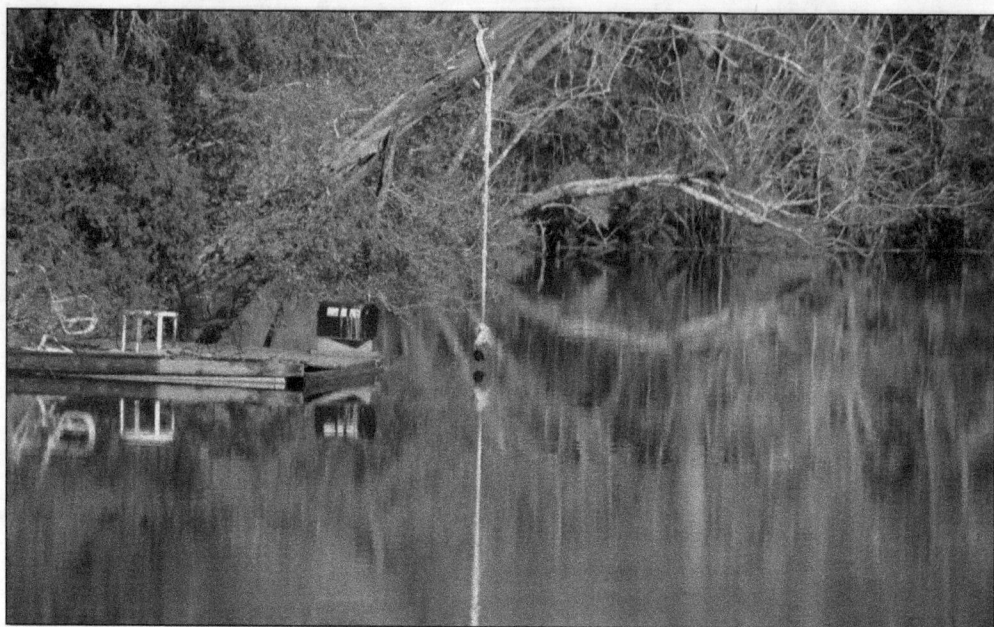

ON THE MAGNOLIA RIVER. Following the river's meandering curves is the beautiful town of Magnolia Springs, developed from an 1800 Spanish land grant; after the end of the War Between the States, many soldiers returned to settle and call it home. Businesses, inns, and homes soon sprang up, welcoming even more transplants from Illinois, Vermont, Missouri, and other railroad stops in the North. (Courtesy of Penny H. Taylor.)

SOUTHLAND SKETCHES   by Walter Overton

POINSETTIAS— BRILLIANT END-OF-THE-YEAR "FLOWER"— AND LATE CHRYSANTHEMUMS— GRACE THE YEAR'S END AND WELCOME IN THE NEW YEAR AT BELLINGRATH GARDENS.

EVERY SEASON AT THE GARDENS HAS ITS OWN FAIRYLIKE CHARM, AND SOMBER WINTER DAYS ARE CHEERFULLY GAY, PRE-SENTING THEIR OWN DELIGHTFUL OFFERINGS OF MULTI-COLORED FOLIAGE AND GORGEOUS MASSES OF BLOSSOMS.

IF YOU REMEMBER THEM LIKE THIS, —YOU'RE AN OLD-TIMER.

THIS EARLY PHONOGRAPH, OWNED BY FRANK SANDERS —FOLEY, ALA, IS A GENUINE MUSICAL ANTIQUE.

FORTY-FIVE SELECTIONS, ON THE CYLINDRICAL WAX RECORDS KNOWN TO THE ESKIMOS AS "CANNED WHITE MAN" HAVE SURVIVED THE YEARS AND CAN STILL BE PLAYED AND BE HEARD AS THEY WERE HEARD LONG YEARS AGO.

BOB HOLK —age 13— MAGNOLIA SPRINGS ALABAMA, SNATCHED AND BOATED 28 MULLET IN LESS THAN AN HOUR,— AN AVERAGE OF ONE MULLET EVERY 2 MIN-UTES.

"SOUTHLAND SKETCHES." Famous Southern artist Walter Overton captured vignettes of easy living in his distinctive series of "Southland Sketches." Illustrating forgotten objects like the early phonograph with wax playback cylinders to native flowers and the ever-present recreational sport of fishing. Catching the "big one" is every fisherman's dream and a fitting end to the chapter. (Courtesy of Baldwin County Department of Archives and History.)

Eight

THE GATEWAY CITY

FOLEY HIGH SCHOOL. The high school building pictured above was built in 1923 and served high school students in a 500-square-mile area. It was built next to the two-story structure on Pine Street. The two-story building served students from grades one through seven, and the new school served high school students from grades eight through twelve. (Courtesy of Penny H. Taylor.)

WORLD WAR I BIVOUAC. Foley was near several military installations. One, Fort Morgan, at the mouth of Mobile Bay, was built from 1819 to 1834. During World War I, a coastal artillery unit of the US Army garrisoned it. Here is pictured the personnel who camped at Foley in preparation for travel to Fort Morgan in 1918. (Courtesy of Foley Library.)

DREDGING THE INTRACOASTAL WATERWAY. In 1935 and 1936, the United States completed digging the canal connecting Mobile Bay and Perdido Bay, providing more efficient ship passage than travel in the rough waters of the Gulf of Mexico. At first, the waterway rounded the bend through Bon Secour Bay, but after many complaints from tugboat pilots, a canal was cut through Plash Island in 1950s. (Courtesy of Swift-Coles Historic Home.)

BARIN FIELD. Barin Field was built in Foley as a naval aviation training facility under the Pensacola command. The field occupied 950 acres, part of which had been the Foley Airport. At completion, the field was an autonomous air station with two sets of runways, four hangars, shops, barracks, offices, and all other support buildings. Pictured above is the tower and main hangar. The SNJ was the training plane, as pictured below. The number of aircraft at the field increased from 111 in December 1942 to more than 400 in April 1944. The first group of 145 flight students entered the facility at its commission on December 5, 1942, one year after the United States entered World War II. (Both, courtesy of Foley Library.)

HURRICANE PREPARATION. After World War II, the field was out of use for a short period but was still used for storage and a landing field. It reopened in 1948 for training purposes and again in 1952 with the outbreak of the Korean War. In preparation for the 1955 hurricane, the wings of these SNJ trainers were folded to prevent as much devastation as possible. The photograph below shows inside the hangar; note the number of the trainers that could be stored efficiently. (Both, courtesy of Foley Museum.)

DIGGING POTATOES. The young men at Barin came from throughout the United States. Thousands of pilots were needed to man the aircraft carriers, which had become the "Queens of the Fleet." For every pilot, there were about 10 support personnel on base for maintenance of the aircraft and providing services for the base. Here are young sailors who have field duty digging potatoes for the kitchen. (Courtesy of Foley Library.)

BASE BASEBALL TEAM. One of the much-needed outlets for those men in "final squadron" training was baseball. The games provided some relief from the pressures placed on them in training. At times, more than 800 pilots were housed and trained at the field, known as "Bloody Barin," as at least 40 young men were killed in the training period. (Courtesy of Foley Library.)

USO CLUB HALL. The Foley Progressive Club was built in 1912 for cultural events and dances. In 1937, it became the American Legion Post No. 99 and was used as the USO Club. During the 1950s, it was the skating rink before it became the Ambrose Hardware. True Value Hardware then operated the business until closing in 1978. At that time, Jackie McLeod renovated the building and opened the Gift Horse Restaurant. (Courtesy of Baldwin County Historical Development Commission.)

AMATEUR NIGHT. The USO in Foley was a large open room that could be put to multiple uses. Pictured is amateur night on August 22, 1944. The sailors were stationed at Barin Field in Foley or at Pensacola Naval Air Station. (Courtesy of Foley Library.)

SATURDAY NIGHT DANCE. Local residents and civilian employees of Barin Field joined to make each event at the USO Club a memorable occasion for the homesick sailors who would soon be sent to the front. Girls came from towns to the north by rail and from the eastern shore of Mobile Bay by bus or automobile. Many local girls met their future husbands at these affairs. (Courtesy of Foley Museum.)

CANTEEN FOR A SODA. The refreshments for events were provided by local citizens. Lemonade and homemade cakes were often served. Most evenings, the music in the hall was played on a Victrola record player, but sometimes, a live band would be hired. (Courtesy of Foley Museum.)

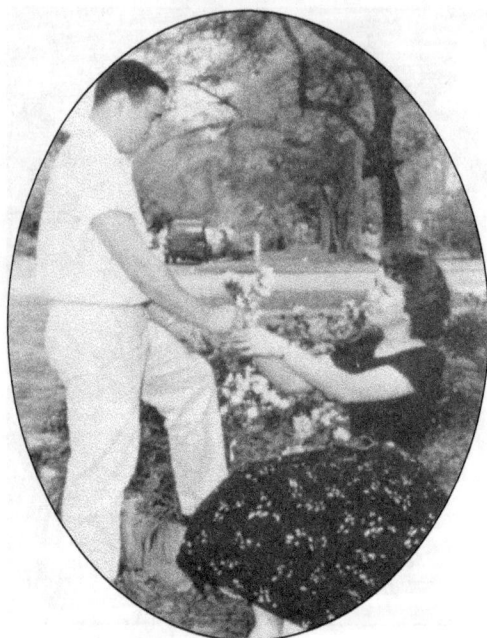

WHO'S WHO AT FOLEY HIGH SCHOOL. The 1950s were stereotypical "Happy Days" in Foley. The class of 1958 elected class favorites pictured above. In the photograph on the left, Jim Donaldson and Norma Simmons were named "Biggest Flirts," and in the photograph on the right, Larry Cole and Bonnie Cleaveland were named "Wittiest." Later, Jim Donaldson and Bonnie Cleaveland were married. (Courtesy of Foley Museum.)

MR. AND MISS FOLEY. Other 1958 class favorites included Mr. and Miss Foley High School, pictured on the left. James Taylor and June Blackmon earned the coveted title. On the right are Nathan Graham and Elsie Medved as "Most Athletic." Elsie Medved and James Taylor were later married. (Courtesy of Foley Museum.)

IVAN JONES ERA. The athletic success during the 1955–1968 tenure of head coach Ivan Jones is legendary. During the five-year span from 1960 through 1964, the Lions had 47 wins and only three defeats. The 1961 team in the photograph above won the Alabama State Championship, as did the 1962 team. Ivan Jones is pictured in the first row on the left. Jones's record was 110-26-3. (Courtesy of Foley Museum.)

SMITH AND FOSTER. Don Foster, pictured on the left, played varsity four years and scored 45 touchdowns. Lester Smith, right, was quarterback for the two championship teams, 1961 and 1962. He followed Ivan Jones as head coach in 1969 and continued the winning tradition with four trips to state playoffs. When he left coaching, he was the winningest coach in county history. Smith and Foster were the first inductees into the Foley High School Hall of Fame in 1984. (Courtesy of Foley Museum.)

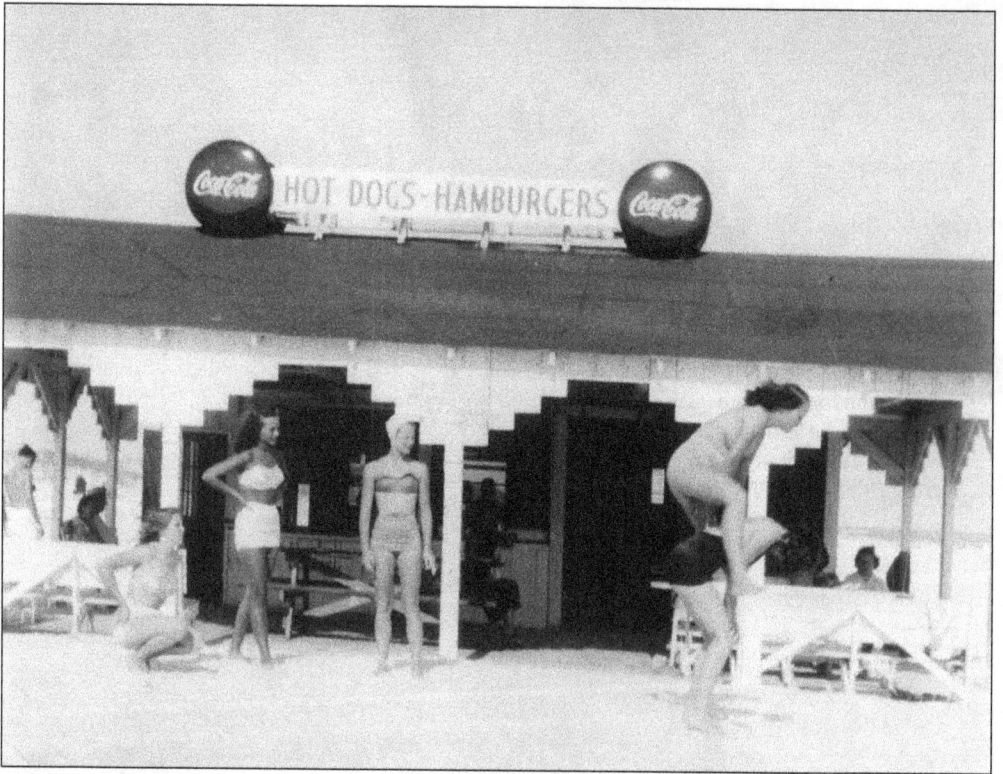

HIGH SCHOOL MEMORIES. Kids Day at the beach was celebrated each year by the senior class. Dressed in kiddie costumes over their swimsuits, they loaded into dump trucks, pickup trucks, and personal vehicles for a day at Gulf Shores. The Little Casino, later known as the Hangout, was the destination for the last fling before graduation. (Both, courtesy of Foley Museum.)

BIBLIOGRAPHY

Baldwin County Heritage Book Committee. *The Heritage of Baldwin County, Alabama*. Clanton, AL: Heritage Publishing Consultants, 2001.

Buskens, Joy Callaway. *Well, I've Never Met a Native*. Columbus, GA: Quill Publications, 1986.

Comings, L.J. and Martha M. Albers. *A Brief History of Baldwin County*. Fairhope, AL: Baldwin County Historical Society, 1928.

England, Jack, Jack Friend, Michael Bailey, and Blanton Blankenship. *Fort Morgan*. Charleston, SC: Arcadia Publishing, 2000.

Lewis, John C. and Harriet Brill Outlaw. *Baldwin County*. Charleston, SC: Arcadia Publishing, 2005.

Magnolia Springs Community Association. *Magnolia Springs Cookbook*. Fairhope, AL: Magnolia Springs Community Association, 1999.

Nuzam, Kay. *A History of Baldwin County*. Bay Minette, AL: *Baldwin Times*, 1971.

Outlaw, Harriet Brill and Penny H. Taylor. *Daphne*. Charleston, SC: Arcadia Publishing, 2011.

Rich, Doris. *When Foley Was Very Young*. Foley, AL: self-published, 1983.

Smith, Robert Leslie. *Gone to the Swamp*. Tuscaloosa: University of Alabama Press, 2008.

Stoddard, Tom. *Foley Steps Forward*. Foley, AL: City of Foley, 2001.

Taylor, June. *Town of Elberta Centennial Celebration, 1904–2004*. Elberta, AL: Elberta Town Council, 2004.

Wakeford, Charley and Meme Wakeford. *Food, Fun, and Fable from Meme's on Bon Secour River*. Bon Secour, AL: self-published, 1965.

Visit us at
arcadiapublishing.com
....

www.ingramcontent.com/pod-product-compliance
Lightning Source LLC
Chambersburg PA
CBHW080632110426
42813CB00006B/1668